SECRET
BUENOS AIRES

Valeria Sampedro and Hernán Firpo

JonGlez

We immensely enjoyed writing the *Secret Buenos Aires* guide and hope that, like us, you will continue to discover the unusual, secret and lesser-known facets of this city.

Accompanying the description of some sites, you will find historical information and anecdotes that will let you understand the city in all its complexity. *Secret Buenos Aires* also sheds light on the numerous yet overlooked details of places we pass by every day. These details are an invitation to pay more attention to the urban landscape and, more generally, to regard our city with the same curiosity and attention we often feel when travelling…

Comments on this guide and its contents, as well as information on sites not mentioned, are welcome and will help us to enrich future editions.

Don't hesitate to contact us:
• Jonglez Publishing,
  17, boulevard du Roi,
  78000 Versailles, France
• E-mail: info@jonglezpublishing.com

p. 124

p. 142

p. 106

p. 12

p. 70

p. 198

p. 214

0   2   4 km

N

Autopista Arturo Illia

Núñez

Av. del Libertador
Av. Monroe
Av. Cabildo

Belgrano

Av. Cabildo

Colegiales

Av. La Cruz

Chacarita

Av. San Martín

Av. Gaona

BUENOS AIRES

Av. Rivadavia
Av. Juan Bautista Alberdi

Av. Varela

Autopista Cámpora

Aeroparque
Jorge Newbery

Jardín
Japonés

Jardín
Zoológico

Palermo Jardín
Botánico

Av. Córdoba

Av. Santa Fe

Biblioteca
Nacional

Recoleta

Estación
Retiro

Retiro

Av. Santa Fe

Av. Córdoba

Av. de los Italianos

Parque
del Centenario

Estación
Once

Almagro

Caballito

Av. Córdoba

Av. Callao

Av. Córdoba

San Nicolás

Plaza del
Congreso

Plaza
de Mayo

Av. Rivadavia

Av. Belgrano

Av. Independencia

Monserrat

Av. La Plata

Av. San Juan

Av. Directorio

Constitución

Estación
Constitución

Boedo

Av. Juan de Garay

Boca

Reg. de Patricios

Parque
Chacabuco

Av. Chiclana

Av. La Plata

Av. Caseros

Av. Vélez Sársfield

Parque de los
Patricios

Av. Cobo

Barracas

Av. Pietro Moreno

Estadio
Pedro Bidegain

Villa
Soldati

Parque
de la
Ciudad

Parque
J. A. Roca

Av. Escalada

Av. Coronel Roca

Av. 27 de Febrero

Valentín
Alsina

Pineyro

RP36

RN1

Av. Hipólito Yrigoyen

Avellaneda

Av. Bartolomé Mitre

Av. Belgrano

LA PLATA

RP14

Gerli

RP36

Villa
Fiorito

Av. General Hornos

Av. General San Martín

Lanús

Autopista Camino Negro

Villa
Centenario

RP210

RP14

CONTENTS

MICRO AND MACRO CENTRO

SAN TELMO AND SURROUNDINGS

CONTENTS

PALERMO AND RECOLETA

EL SUR

CENTRE

CENTRE WEST

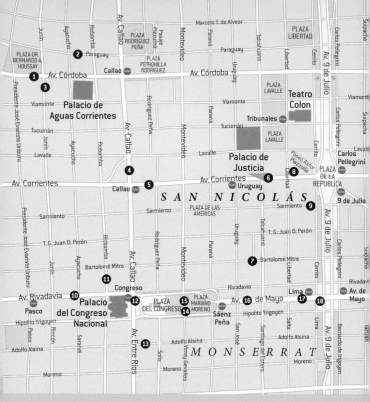

MICRO AND MACRO CENTRE

PEDIMENT OF THE *FACULTAD DE CIENCIAS ECONÓMICAS* ❶

2122 Avenida Cordoba
Metro: line D, Faculty of Medicine station; line B, Pasteur station

> *A medical scene for accountants and economists*

The plaster relief that decorates the tympanum of the pediment on the Faculty of Economic Sciences is far from being representative of the subjects taught within its walls today. It shows a hospital scene with an operating table, a patient, doctors, students and skulls. In fact, the building was originally built to house the Faculty of Medicine.

Francesco Tamburini (1846–1891) – an Italian architect who was also behind the original construction project for the Teatro Colón and the final stages of the work on the Casa Rosada – was commissioned by the State to build the faculty. It was inaugurated in 1908 for the School of Medical Sciences and the Institute of Forensic Science. It rapidly became overcrowded, however, and in 1945 a new building was erected. It is easy to imagine the raised eyebrows when the aspiring economists and public accountants who then moved into the building were faced with sharing the same premises as the morgue … which continued to be housed in the part of the building looking out onto Calle Viamonte.

THE CREMATORIUM CHIMNEY

If you glance through the windows that look out onto the central patio, you will see an enormous brick chimney stack which was used to evacuate the air from the crematorium at the time.

It is said that, in the 1960s, when the police stormed the faculty in search of some militant students, the students in question fled down the secret passages linking the two buildings.

The metro stop on line D just opposite the entrance to the university, at No. 2100 on Avenida Cordoba, is still called Faculty of Medicine today. When the Buenos Aires metro was opened, medicine was still being taught there even if the move from one building to the other had already been planned.

MUSEO DE LA GLORIA AJEDRECÍSTICA

1858 Calle Paraguay
- Metro: line D, Callao or Facultad de Medicina station
- Open daily 5pm—midnight. Free admission

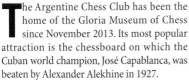

A reference to the game between Alekhine and Capablanca

The Argentine Chess Club has been the home of the Gloria Museum of Chess since November 2013. Its most popular attraction is the chessboard on which the Cuban world champion, José Capablanca, was beaten by Alexander Alekhine in 1927.

There are also original paintings and photos of this mythical match, signed by iconic figures like Karpov and Kasparov, among others.

The aim of the museum is to promote Russia's world-renowned passion for the game in Argentina. It is a demonstration of the close ties that exist between the two countries as it was born out of a joint project run by the gallery and the House of Russia.

On display are many letters written and photos taken by Alekhine during his stay in Argentina, in addition to photos of Kasparov's arrival before a crowd of more than 5,000 fans.

As visitors walk through the museum, they are taken on a voyage through the history of chess, interspersed with information about the game's key figures.

The Gloria Museum of Chess is a highly symbolic place for Russians as

it was in this very place that the first Russian world champion was declared.

The "Duel of the Century Room" portrays another mythical game which took place during the Cold War between Bobby Fischer and Tigran Petrosian.

The American defeated the Russian in the semi-final of the 1971 World Championships.

Toy shops in Buenos Aires that stocked chess games were all sold out.

MUSEUM OF THE INSTITUTO DE CIENCIAS FORENSES

Forensic Sciences Institute
760 Calle Junin
• Metro: line D, Facultad de Medecina station; line B, Pasteur station
• Visits: Mon—Fri 9am—3pm. Free admission

I n the 1920s the Institute of Forensic Sciences set up a museum: it was designed to provide medical and legal training to students of the National School of Police, the military police and the Prefecture, in addition to the staff working for the penitentiary administration.

Employees have had to resuscitate visitors on more than one occasion ...

The museum is open to the public but, if you are squeamish, you had better give this visit a miss. There are human remains, photos and plaster casts on display, and visitors can learn to distinguish between different types of wounds found on the bodies of people who have had their throats cut or who have cut their own throats in order to commit suicide.

Other rooms explain the trajectory of bullets and stab wounds, and have anatomical reproductions of bodies that have been opened up. Even the head of Rogelio Gordillo, a famous criminal who was killed during a shoot-out with the police, is on display here. The museum staff explain that, "The aim of the museum is not to frighten people, but for them to try and learn something from death." In practice, they have had to resuscitate visitors on more than one occasion ...

One of the museum sections has showcases displaying the dangers of children playing with small objects and putting them in their mouths: there are larynxes obstructed by marbles, coins or grapes. Visitors can also see many different ways of carrying illicit substances: they have been hidden in bars of soap, tennis balls, and sports shoes with double-lined soles, to name but a few. They show just how ingenious criminals can be.

BUENOS AIRES' TWO STATUES OF LIBERTY

450 Avenida Callao
• Metro: lines B and D, Callao station

> *Inaugurated*
> *25 days before*
> *its famous twin*

You may have noticed the little red Statue of Liberty standing on the Barrancas de Belgrano (see box) on Avenida 11 de Septiembre and Calle La Pampa. If so, you will be surprised to hear that Buenos Aires possesses another exact replica, which can be seen standing high on the front of a college at No. 450 in Avenida Callao. What is perhaps even more surprising is that it was inaugurated twenty-five days before its famous North American twin.

The Buenos Aires statue is the work of the Italian architect Carlos Morra, who was commissioned to design the then National Library, and the Domingo Faustino Sarmiento College, which was to open its doors on 3 October 1886.

On the following 28 October, what is today known as "the" Statue of Liberty was unveiled on the southern side of Manhattan. This gift from the people of France to mark the centenary of American Independence was not just a happy coincidence. Its famous sculptor, Frédéric Auguste Bartholdi, made several scaled-down models before attempting to cast the enormous full-size statue. It is thought that this is how one of the moulds was used to make a replica for the front of the college in Buenos Aires ...

The statue also has a symbolic side to it, making reference to the Masonic master, Sarmiento, as Bartholdi's work uses the signs for Knowledge and the Sun common to Freemasonry.

The statue in Barrancas de Belgrano was ordered from France by the city of Buenos Aires and placed on a stone pedestal. Those who take a closer look (while keeping off the lawn around it) will be in for a surprise as they read the following inscription: "Cast by Le Val d'Osne68, 8 rue Voltaire, Paris. A. Bartholdi". So it really is an original.

The Barrancas de Belgrano are sloping plots of land which make up the Plaza Barrancas de Belgrano today.

ALBERTO OLMEDO'S HANDPRINTS

1753 Avenida Corrientes
• Metro: line B, Callao station
• Buses: 12, 24, 29, 60, 102, 168

A lberto Olmedo, aka "El Negro Olmedo" (1933–1988), was a famous Argentinian comic and actor from Mar del Plata. His death (he fell from a balcony during a party) caused a great outpouring of emotion.

A statue of my hands

One day, during an interview, a journalist asked him what he would like to leave behind when he died. He was quoted as saying: "A statue of my hands, on Avenida Corrientes, so that people will remember me as they walk past." After his death, many tributes were paid to him and his wish was granted: on Avenida Corrientes, just before it crosses Avenida Callao, there is a small brick column with a bronze plaque at the top, bearing Olmedo's two handprints together with his photo.

Unfortunately, both the plaque and the photo were stolen and in 2009 the Friends of Avenida Corrientes Association moved the monument to No. 1753 on the avenue. It now stands on the pavement in front of the old Alfil Cine-Theatre, where the actor performed his final season in Buenos Aires.

In November 2010, the city of Buenos Aires erected a statue of "El Negro Olmedo" and his gambling partner, Javier Portales, at the intersection of Avenidas Corrientes and Uruguay. The unveiling of the statue caused quite a stir as there was some confusion, among members of the Friends of Avenida Corrientes Association, as to whether the new statue had been installed without taking into account the existence of the first … or whether it was just a way for the mayor of Buenos Aires, Mauricio Macri, to express his admiration for Olmedo.

Today, the two statues stand within a few metres of each other.

ANACHRONISM OF THE MURAL IN AVENIDA CORRIENTES ❻

1369 Avenida Corrientes
• Metro: line B, Uruguay station; line D, Tribunales station

> ## Carlos Gardel never saw the Obelisk

The awning of Los Inmortales (The Immortals) Pizzeria, one of the traditional pizzerias on Avenida Corrientes, is decorated with a mural, or rather an advertisement, dating back to the 1950s and showing Carlos Gardel.

The tango dancer is shown standing, dressed in a black coat and top hat and holding a cane and white gloves. In the background we can see the hustle and bustle of a city "that never sleeps", with its buses, its buildings, the pizzeria and … the Obelisk.

If we were to stop for a moment and consider the area's chronological development, we would see that Carlos Leonetti, the painter of this mural, has

taken the liberty of including an anachronism. Gardel died on 24 June 1935 whereas the Obelisk was inaugurated 11 months later, after only 60 working days.

The work is based on a famous image of Gardel from *Tango Bar*, the last film that the singer appeared in. The mural on Avenida Corrientes (38 metres wide x 2.10 metres high) was inaugurated on the terrace of the pizzeria shortly after it opened, to commemorate the twentieth anniversary of Gardel's tragic death.

At the back of the pizzeria, above the counter, customers can see a smaller version of the work in addition to a selection of old photos of Gardel.

ANOTHER "MISTAKE"
The trained eye may catch another oddity in the mural: the artist has changed the direction of the traffic on the avenue – a small detail perhaps for this work, considering that it has never enjoyed critical acclaim.

PASAJE RIVAROLA

1330 Bartolomé Mitre
- Metro: line A, Sáenz Peña station
- Buses: 5, 7, 98, 105

> *A perfectly symmetrical, 100-year-old passage*

Pasaje Rivarola, which runs through a block of houses on Calles Talcahuano, Uruguay, Perón and Mitre, is rather special: both sides are identical. The doors, balconies, domes and windows were all made to be perfectly symmetrical.

The buildings are all five storeys high and those standing at the four ends of the road have domes.

They also have patios and are extremely well constructed, using bronze, fine wrought-iron work and classical trimmings.

Once inside, you can see marble landings and hear the characteristic sound of old-fashioned lifts, with their collapsible metal gates, carrying residents up and down.

In spite of its considerable age (it is around 100 years old), it feels as if the passage was built recently as it is in such good condition. Indeed, it has often been used as a backdrop for films and advertisements.

Until the 1950s, it was called "Pasaje Rural" as it was built on a plot where an insurance company of that name had once stood.

In later years, these office buildings were gradually bought up and converted

into flats. In the sixties, the name was changed to "Pasaje Rivarola".

There is an imposing clock hanging at the entrance to the passage, a souvenir of the time when a shop called The Clock Cemetery sold all manner of clocks. It even stocked the soft, melting clocks made popular by Salvador Dali's famous work. There was a time when clock-lovers came from far and wide to admire rare collector's items here.

STATUES IN EL VESUVIO ICE-CREAM PARLOUR ❽

1181 Avenida Corrientes
• Metro: lines B, C, Pellegrini station; line D, Tribunales station

" A homage to tango, hidden away on the first floor of an ice-cream parlour

When you step into El Vesuvio ice-cream parlour, you will no doubt be surprised to see a clock, decorated with famous figures from the world of tango, hanging on one of the walls. There is also a series of statuettes on the first floor representing the musicians Aníbal Carmelo (aka "Gordo") Trolio (1914–1975), Roberto Goyeneche (1926–1994) and Carlos Gardel (1890–1935). This tribute to three icons of Argentinian tango was created by Paula Franzi, a sculptor who trained at the National School of Fine Arts.

Behind the shop is an area where a collection of works inspired by tango is on permanent display.

The reason why tango has such an important place in El Vesuvio's decor is that the ice-cream parlour, which has been there since 1902, is mentioned in a tango song entitled *La Última Grela*. It was composed by Astor Piazzola and Horacio Ferrer, who were regular customers, together with Carlos Gardel and Jorge Luis Borges.

El Vesuvio was one of the very first ice-cream parlours to be set up in Buenos Aires. The Cocitores, a family of Italian immigrants, were the first to import a manual ice-cream-making machine. At the time, two employees were needed to work the handle of the enormous, manually operated, metal cylinder. Over the years, El Vesuvio began offering a wider range of products to its customers, with the addition of sweets and *churros*. These sidelines enabled it to remain open throughout the year.

El Vesuvio's stained-glass windows, showing a smoking volcano, split up the rays of daylight coming into the shop and are considered a real work of art. The shop has been declared a Site of Public Interest in Buenos Aires, and in 2006 a commemorative plaque was unveiled there to thank the establishment for its contribution to the city's cultural identity.

CHALET ON AVENIDA 9 DE JULIO ⑨

1113 Calle Sarmiento, Microcentro district
• Metro: line B, Carlos Pellegrini station; line D, Avenida 9 de Julio station;
line C, Diagonal Norte station

A chalet perched high on top of a building

Look up beyond the Obelisk of Buenos Aires and you will see a strange chalet perched high on the top of a building. The man who put it up there in 1927 was a well-known Spanish furniture maker called Rafael Diaz.

Apparently, he wanted it built in the same style as his house in Mar del Plata.

When Diaz bought the building and moved in to set up his shop, he had this little house built so that he could sneak away there for his daily afternoon nap from 2 to 4pm.

In the 1930s, Diaz boasted that he could see the Uruguayan coast and the town of Colonia from there.

He also had a great view of the construction of the Obelisk in 1936. He installed an antenna on the roof of the building – with his name written on it in enormous letters – when he set up his very own radio station to play music and advertise his company.

However, when radio broadcasting began to be regulated, he refused to pay his licence and sold his broadcasting frequency.

Sadly, today we can no longer see the Uruguayan coast from the chalet as billboards have long since obscured the view.

The little house is now home to the building's administrative offices. Nevertheless, its originality lies in the tiled roof, the bow windows so characteristic of English films, and the magnificent arabesques decorating the floor.

After Diaz died, the chalet was handed down to his children and then to his grandchildren.

DOME OF THE *"NO HI HA SOMNIS IMPOSSIBLES"* BUILDING

🔟

2009 Avenida Rivadavia, Balvanera district
• Metro: line A, Congreso station

*A homage
to Antoni Gaudí*

The Balvanera district, at the crossroads of Calles Rivadavia and Ayacucho, has a distinctly Catalan flavour: one of the finest and most typical domes in Buenos Aires can be found here. You might at first think that it is the work of Antoni Gaudí, but you would be wrong. It was in fact designed by the engineer Rodriguez Ortega, a fervent admirer of the Catalan architect.

The building, which was inaugurated in 1914, has a ground floor, a mezzanine, four floors of apartments and a terrace measuring 350m². At the very top is a small, onion-shaped dome, with an iron weathervane.

In 1999 the architect Fernando Lorenzi, an expert on Gaudí, undertook the restoration of the building. After a considerable amount of in-depth historical research, he had metal girders installed to support the lateral balconies, copied to scale from those on the famous dragon's gate in the Güell Pavilions in Barcelona. Some of the details are identical to those on the Casa Batlló. It took 952 pieces of polished glass to cover the dome. The building is named after the inscription in Catalan on the front, which reads *"No hi ha somnis impossibles"* (There is no such thing as an impossible dream).

NEARBY

CASA DE LOS LIRIOS
2013 Avenida Rivadavia
• Metro: line A, Congreso station

Rodríguez Ortega's work, the so-called Palace of the Irises (because the front is covered in sculpted, flame-like flowers), is a fine example of Art Nouveau.

The terrace has a fresco made out of fish scales running along the moulding, with a gargoyle representing a Greek god in the centre.

The building is being looked after by the city council until it is officially listed as a Historical Monument.

THE "PALM HOUSE"

100 Calle Riobamba
• Metro: line A, Congreso station
• Buses: 2, 95, 60, 64, 86

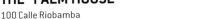

The legend of a haunted house said to have inspired Cortázar

The first short story by Julio Cortázar (see box) to be published, *Casa Tomada* (House Taken Over), tells the story of a brother and sister who gradually abandon the rooms in their house after hearing disturbing noises which lead them to believe that they are haunted. Strangely, this story recalls the mysterious tale of the "Palm House", which owes its name to the tree obscuring its facade.

Located close to the Argentine National Congress, this French-style residence was occupied two centuries ago by the rich Lady Catalina Espinosa de Galcerán, her husband and six children: five boys and a girl, Elisa. After Catalina's death, her children decided to leave her bedroom untouched and lock the room.

Each of the brothers received a share of the family's considerable fortune, which allowed them to live comfortably without needing to work or study. Although the five boys benefited greatly from their situation, Elisa was incensed at the unfairness of it.

What we know for certain is that, after the death of their mother, the five brothers died one after the other in strange circumstances and within a short period of time. As they each passed away, Elisa locked the doors to their rooms, so that nobody would be able to enter. She then continued to live alone for forty years and died in the basement of the abandoned house. The house itself remained shut for several years until, somewhat ironically, it was acquired by the "Open Doors School". Some time later, the residence was occupied by the Institute of Socialist Thought, but both these initiatives were very short-lived.

Although some commentators claim that the story of this strange house served as the inspiration for Cortázar's short story, other sources maintain that the theme of *Casa Tomada* is no more than an anti-Peronist allegory.

The house remains unoccupied today: seemingly on the verge of collapse, it is still steeped in mystery, as in Cortázar's tale.

Julio Cortázar (born Jules Florencio Cortázar; 1914–1984) was an Argentinian writer, the author of many novels and short stories in Spanish, in which the fantastical and the surreal are recurrent themes. An opponent of the Perón government, in 1951 he emigrated to France, where he lived until his death.

REPLICAS OF THE LOLA MORA SCULPTURES ⑫

National Congress
50 Avenida Entre Rios
• Metro: line A, Congreso station
• Buses: 6, 12, 37, 50, 150

> ***Forbidden for over 90 years***

Two mysterious statues decorate either side of the central staircase on the front of the Legislative Palace: they are two of Lola Mora's masterpieces (see opposite).

The Argentinian artist was commissioned by parliament to sculpt the two statues in white stone; they were erected in

1907. One represents Liberty, Progress and two lions, and the other, Justice, Work and Peace.

But the work was severely criticised by the conservatives when it was unveiled as it showed the naked bust of a woman and was said to be an insult to the very memory of those it claimed to honour.

The sculptures were therefore removed and put in storage until 1921, when they were given to the Province of Jujuy, which placed them in the grounds of its main administrative offices.

Ninety-three years went by before the sculptures (or rather, their replicas)

were put back in their original setting. As the Province of Jujuy refused to give the statues back to the State, President Cristina Fernandez de Kirchner had no alternative but to have copies made. Polyurethane moulds were created using 3D digital drawings of the originals; a mixture of ground marble, white cement and reinforced concrete was poured into these moulds. The different parts were then assembled and in March 2014, the two sculptures were finally put back in their original location.

LOLA MORA, THE CONTROVERSIAL ARTIST

Dolores Candelaria Mora Vega, born in Tucuman in 1866, was Argentina's first female sculptor.

She skilfully cultivated her scandalous image by fuelling rumours about herself. She was rebellious.

She would wear trousers, climb scaffolding and sculpt naked bodies that shocked the more conservative members of society at that time. Mora was bisexual and President Julio A. Roca's mistress.

At the age of 43, she got married to a man who was 20 years her junior. She failed in her attempt to join the Freemasons, as she was a woman.

Her most famous work, the Las Nereidas Fountain, also caused a stir because of the naked nymphs emerging from the water. The fountain was therefore tucked away in a small square behind the Casa Rosada, to silence its detractors, instead of being put in the centre of the Plaza de Mayo, for where it had originally been designed.

SOLDI CANVAS OF THE ARGENTINIAN ACTORS ⓭ ASSOCIATION

Argentinian Actors Association (AAA)
1766 Calle Adolfo Alsina
• Metro: line A, Congreso station
Buses: 2, 37, 60, 86, 105, 150

> **Soldi began his career by painting cinema curtains**

There is a huge painting by one of Argentina's most famous painters, Raúl Soldi (1905–1994), in the Argentinian Actors Association headquarters. Entitled *Alegoría* (Allegory), it evokes the spirit of scenic art.

This oil painting, measuring 5 x 2 metres, has found its way here because Soldi was close to the world of acting – he worked for some time as a set designer and a painter of cinema curtains.

In the 1940s Soldi was greatly inspired by actors, dancers, jugglers, trapeze artists and all manner of figures from the worlds of circus and the theatre. This influence can be seen in works such as *Pierrot and Blanco* and *El Más albañil de los colores.*

Alegoría seems to be an extension of *Alegoría de la música, del canto y del baile* (Allegory of Music, Singing and Dance) (1965), which covers one of the domes of the Teatro Colón. In this fresco, fifty-one figures move around in a colourful whirl of ballets, operas, concerts and orchestras. If, as an art critic once said, Soldi's work is a "repetition of charms", the wall of the Argentinian Actors Association certainly reveals the painter's view of life.

In order to capture the magic of the theatre, Soldi strove to use a wide pallet of colours for the different characters: "When I started working on the original project, I thought about what could have happened or what had actually happened on the stage. This is how I imagined the spiral composed of fifty-one figures, including some of the divinities of the theatre that I managed to add in each corner."

RODIN'S *THE THINKER*

⑭

Plaza Moreno, Congreso district
• Metro: line A, Congreso station
• Buses: 8, 12, 39, 86, 146, 168

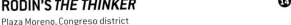

*One
of three original
reproductions*

Plaza Moreno, which runs alongside Plaza Congreso and forms part of the gardens opposite the National Congress building, has been home to one of the original sculptures of Rodin's *The Thinker* for 100 years: a man sits alone, deep in reflection. You may well be thinking, where are the hoards of tourists jostling each other to get a photo or lost in admiration before such perfection? The fact is that very few people know that this patinated bronze statue is one of three original reproductions of the most famous of Rodin's works cast in the original mould.

This famous sculpture is part of the *Gates of Hell* work created by the French artist in 1880 and inspired by Dante's *Divine Comedy*. Rodin first made a tiny plaster cast and said that the man represented in his sculpture was not only thinking with his head but with his whole body. He then cast the statue on a much larger scale and it was unveiled to the public in 1904.

Rodin personally made two copies from the original mould and signed them. The first is on display at the Rodin Museum in Paris; the second is in Philadelphia, USA. The reproduction in Buenos Aires was acquired in 1907 by the director of the National Museum of Fine Arts, Eduardo Schiaffino, who intended to place it on the steps leading up to the National Congress building. Unfortunately, the statue was instead taken to Plaza Moreno and left there, out of sight.

An employee in a hotel on one side of the square remarked: "If tourists ask me what there is to be seen here, I tell them to cross over the road and go and see *The Thinker*." In spite of the statue's significance for the city's cultural heritage, it remains sorely unacknowledged.

ONE OF THE CITY'S TWO PROTECTED MONUMENTS

As it was displayed in the open air, *The Thinker* was vandalized several times until the government decided to place it in a glass enclosure a few years ago. The only other monument that has this kind of protection is the Nereid Fountain.

KILOMETRE ZERO ⑮

Plaza Mariano Moreno, Plaza del Congreso
Calle Virrey Ceballos, Avenidas Hipolito Yrigoyen and Rivadavia
• Metro: line A, Sáenz Peña station

> *The starting point of Argentinian roads*

A 2 metre-high carved block of stone representing Kilometre Zero, from where all road distances in Argentina are measured, can be found in the very last of the squares opposite the Argentine National Congress, between Avenidas Hipolito Yrigoyen and Rivadavia and at the beginning of Calle Virrey Ceballos.

Do not expect to see anything architecturally remarkable. The monolith – created by the sculptors Maximo Fioravanti and his more famous brother, José – is one of the lesser-known sculptures in the square. In spite of its significance, tourists and locals alike walk past it without a glance. It is outshone by the avenue's huge centrepiece: the fountain, the bronze horses and Rodin's *The Thinker* (see p. 39).

It is really worth a closer look. The southern side is carved with a map of Argentina; the northern side has a ceramic mosaic representing the Lujan Virgin, patron saint of the Republic. The monument also pays tribute to Don José de Saint Martin, a national hero.

The milestone was laid in 1935, when General Agustin Pedro was in power. In addition to his military role, the general was an engineer and had a keen interest in road construction. This is why Kilometre Zero was erected on 5 October, known as "Road Day".

But why was it erected in Plaza del Congresso? It is said that the choice of this location is symbolic. The origins of road planning go way back to Ancient Rome, when the Emperor Caesar Augustus had the *Milliarium Aureum* (Golden Milestone) column built. It symbolised the starting point of all the roads in his empire and was located in the Roman Forum, where public affairs were discussed.

A few years ago a wire fence was put up around the Kilometre Zero monument and the other sculptures in the square to protect them from pilfering and numerous acts of vandalism.

SYMBOLISM OF THE PALACIO BAROLO

1370 Avenida de Mayo
- Metro: line C, Avenida de Mayo station; line A, Sáenz Peña station
- Guided tours: Mon, Thurs and Sat (night-time tours possible). Advance booking essential on +54 11 4831-1885
- Visits without a guide: Mon–Fri during office hours (building open to the public)

> **An allegory of The Divine Comedy**

The Barolo Palace is not only one of the most beautiful buildings in Buenos Aires, it is also the city's only allegory of *The Divine Comedy*, the chef-d'oeuvre of Dante Alighieri (1265–1321).

The man who was commissioned to construct this building was the famous Italian architect Mario Palanti (1885–1978). He also designed the Palacio Roccatagliata (Avenidas Santa Fe and Callao); the iconic Pasaje Barolo on Avenida de Mayo; and the Palacio Alcorta, which was once the home of the car dealer Fevre & Basset, with its test track on the roof, and now hosts the Renault museum.

The structure of the Barolo Palace mirrors the literary structure of Dante's famous poem. The palace is 100 metres high, representing the 100 cantos, while its 22 floors represent the 22 verses of the work. Each floor was then divided into 11 modules, which were in turn divided individually into 22 offices. These two numbers are considered to be the sacred symbols of the circle, the perfect figure, according to Dante and the Pythagorean school of thought: the number 22 represents the elementary movements of Aristotelian physics, whereas the number 11 symbolises the Fedeli d'Amore, a religious order to which Dante belonged.

The building is also divided into three parts, as is the book itself: Inferno, Purgatory and Paradise. On the ground floor there are nine vaults, built along a central passage: they represent the nine infernal hierarchies and are decorated with gargoyles and snakes in addition to Latin inscriptions. The inscriptions are taken from nine different texts of Virgil's bible. The floors above (from the first to the fourteenth) symbolise the atonement of sins. The tower at the very top, stretching upwards and away from the solid mass of the building, is crowned by a light to represent God.

The dome is similar to those found on Hindu temples in the Bhubaneshwar region on the east coast of India. If you visit the palace, the guide will probably tell you how the temples represented love and that the dome, in a very similar style, was built to symbolise the bond between the poet Dante and Beatrice, the woman he loved.

WHY IS THE SOUTHERN CROSS IN LINE WITH THE LIGHT ON THE PALACE DURING THE FIRST DAYS OF JUNE?

In *The Divine Comedy*, Dante states that the Southern Cross is the door to Paradise. Palanti therefore calculated the position of the light so that it would be in line with the constellation on the first days of June, to coincide with Dante's birthday.

For further information about Dante and the esotericism in *The Divine Comedy*, see pp. 46–47.

A SECRET PLAN TO RETRIEVE DANTE'S ASHES

Specialists on the Barolo Palace and its occult symbolism support the theory that there was a plan to retrieve Dante's remains so that they could be kept in the building.

Although there is no written proof of this scheme, the story goes that the mysterious death of Luis Barolo in 1922, a year before the building of his dreams was inaugurated, could be linked to the strange disappearance of a sculpture showing Dante going up to Paradise. Instead of having it made in his studio in Buenos Aires, Palanti is said to have travelled to Italy, where he sculpted the work himself and then brought it back.

Rumour has it that the poet's ashes were hidden inside it and that the sculpture was stolen once the secret was revealed.

DANTE, THE TEMPLARS AND *I FEDELI D'AMORE*

The age of Dante Alighieri (1265-1321) was profoundly marked by the decline of the Order of the Knights Templars, and above all by the series of persecutions, imprisonments and condemnations to which the Order was subjected following its interdiction by the king of France, Philip IV, and Pope Clement V (clearly manipulated by the former). These events had a powerful impact upon Dante, who denounced this injustice before the political powers of the day. He went so far as to take part in an event in Florence that was a deliberate expression of support for Pope Boniface VIII, who in 1302 had been denounced as a heretic by the *États Généraux* summoned by Philip IV; in 1303, the king sent his troops to Florence to hold the pontiff prisoner in Palazzo d'Agnani for three days. The Templars, who were the pope's personal guard, were on this occasion supported by the local burghers, including Dante, and managed to free Pope Boniface VIII. However, he died just a month later in rather unclear circumstances; some even mentioned poison. Philip IV supported the immediate election of Clement V and set about persecuting the Templars, ultimately procuring their total destruction – in spite of the fact that a delegation (of which Dante was a part) had gone to Rome to argue their case before the pope in 1307. It is thought that Dante's initiation into the social and religious ideals underpinning the Templars came when he frequented their Florentine headquarters at San Jacopo, in Campo Corbolini. In this area, the Templars are credited with the original construction of the church of San Jacopo Sopr'Arno.

The Order aimed to promote, within the Christian faith and thence society as a whole, their ideal of spiritual perfection and temporal justice. To this end, they used poetry, song and the prose works of the Confraternity of Troubadours, advocates of a philosophy of "spiritual love" who were continually at loggerheads with the dominion exerted by Rome. Dante himself was one of these *Fedeli d'Amore* [The Faithful of Love].

The Confraternity of troubadours and minstrels had spread throughout the whole of Europe. The first traces of it are to be found in the poetry of the tenth and eleventh centuries, in courtly praise to the Mother of God and celebrations of the blessings of humanity. In a sense the descendants of the ancient *vates* (soothsayers) and bards, the troubadours wrote under the guidance of important spiritual masters, producing love songs and satirical lyrics that expressed esoteric truths. In short, they might be described as the "mouthpiece" of the different esoteric Orders that then existed in Europe, and there was a profound relation between their poetry and the kind of spirituality championed by the Templars.

Disgusted by the bloody destruction of the Order of the Knights Templars, Dante wanted to set the record straight for future generations, giving a masterly explication of its true aims in his literary masterpiece *La Divina Commedia*. It is interesting, for example, that in his *Paradiso*, from the third heaven inwards the poet is guided through the heavens towards his vision of God by St. Bernard of Clairvaux, who had been the spiritual father of the Templars. Similarly, when he reaches the highest of the heavens, the poet rediscovers Beatrice, his beloved and the expression of divine grace. There he has a vision of a white rose with a triangle at its centre; the latter symbolises love of the Holy Trinity, whilst the rose itself had been a symbol adopted by the *Fedeli d'Amore*.

The very decision to write the poem in the vernacular — the local dialect of *Toscan*, which is very close to modern-day Italian — was a gesture of revolt against Rome and its ecclesiastical Latin. It is also significant that in the eighth circle of hell called *Maleboge* (Fraud), Dante places two popes: Boniface VIII, condemned for simony (the sale of ecclesiastical honours) and Clement V, the corrupt pope who signed the condemnation of the Templars.

A "comedy" not because it is comic but because it ends well for all the characters who gain admission to Heaven, *La Divina Commedia* is made up of 100 *canti* and a total of 14,233 lines. Its three parts (*Paradiso, Purgatorio* and *Inferno*) are each made up of 33 *canti* of 40 to 50 tercets (verses of three lines). The *Inferno* also has an introductory *canto*, thus bringing the total of *canti* to 100; a symbol of absolute perfection ($100=10 \times 10 =$ the perfection of that which is perfect), this number is also to be found, for example, in the 100 names of the God of Islam. Each *canto* is made up of 130 to 140 lines of *terza rima* (that is, interlocking tercets). Thus, one continually finds multiples of the numbers 3, 7 and 10, all of which were heavily symbolic in the Middle Ages and might be taken to express the poet's devotion to the Holy Trinity, a special object of devotion for the Templars themselves.

Terza rima here involves hendecasyllabic lines (11 syllables) organised in rhymes that follow the schema ABA, BCB, CDC, EDE, and so on, with the central line of one tercet rhyming with the first and third of the following one. This structure is also known as "Dante's tercet", because he was the first to use it. Furthermore, the three books of the *Commedia* all end in a rhyme on the same word: *Stelle* (stars). It should be remembered that Mary, the mother of Christ, was often referred to as *Stella Maris* and again was an object of particular devotion for the Templars.

BEATRICE: A SYMBOL OF THE PATH OF SPIRITUAL ENLIGHTENMENT

Dante says he met Beatrice when he was 18 years old, even if he had first noticed her when he was nine and she eight. Some argue that he only saw her once and that he never even spoke to her. There is no biographical evidence to prove the matter one way or another.

Solely on the basis of the biographical information that Dante himself supplies in *La Vita Nuova*, we know that Beatrice (Bice) Portinari was born in 1265-66 and died on 8 June 1290. She has been identified as the daughter of the banker Folco Portinari from Portico di Romagna, who left her a substantial sum of money in his will dated 1287. We also know that Beatrice married the Florentine nobleman Simone de Bardi, by whom she had six daughters, and lived in a house next to Dante's in Florence. She founded the Ospedale di Santa Maria Nuova, today the hospital of central Florence.

Dante's dithyrambic praise of her Christian charity has immortalised her as *Beata Beatrice* [Blessed Beatrice]; it was under this name that Dante Gabriel Rossetti painted her in 1864, in a picture which shows the dove of the Holy Spirit appearing to her whilst carrying a rose in its beak.

The rose was the symbol of the *Fedeli d'Amore* (see p. 47) and also the flower of spiritual enlightenment and revelation. This is why the Litany of the Blessed Virgin Mary mentions a "mystic rose".

The courtly love of the twelfth and thirteenth century – for the first time since the Gnostics of the second and third century – glorified the spiritual dignity and religious virtue of women. Gnostic texts, for example, had exulted the Mother of God at the same time as the "mystical silence" of the Holy Spirit and the Wisdom of God.

If medieval devotions to the Virgin were an indirect veneration of women, Dante went one step further: he deified Beatrice, proclaiming her as superior to the angels and saints, as invulnerable to sin and almost comparable to the Virgin herself. Thus, when Beatrice is about to appear within the Earthly Paradise, a voice proclaims: "Come, O my spouse, from Lebanon" (*Purgatorio*, XXX, 11) – a famous line from the *Song of Songs* (IV, 8) which had been used by the Church in its veneration of the Mother of God.

In another passage (*Purgatorio*, XXXIII, 10), Beatrice applies to herself words that had first been used by Christ: "A little while, and ye shall not see me; and again, a little while, and ye shall see me." (John 16.16)

Beatrice represents Wisdom and thus the mystery of Salvation; Dante introduces her during the course of his three journeys of initiation into Hell, Purgatory and Heaven. She is presented as the idealisation of the Eternal Woman, the chosen means of communication that can lead to the metaphysical re-awakening and salvation of humankind.

This view of love and the veneration of womanhood as playing a part in the salvation of the human soul inspired the gnosis and esoteric initiations of the *Fedeli d'Amore* – as one can see in *La Vita Nuova* [New Life], which Dante dedicates to Beatrice. Written in 1292-93, this work describes initiation through spiritual love, with the figure of Woman being a symbol of *Intellectus illuminatio*, of the transcendent Spirit and Divine Wisdom that are destined to awaken the Christian world from the lethargy to which it has succumbed as a result of the spiritual ignobility of the popes. Thus, in the medieval writings of the *Fedeli d'Amore* one finds allusions to "a widow who is not such". This was the *Madonna Intelligenza*, who had become a "widow" because her spouse – the pope – was dead to the spiritual, having given himself over entirely to temporal affairs and corruption.

The veneration of the "Unique Woman" – and initiation into the mysteries of Love – were part of what made the *Fedeli d'Amore* into a sort of secret spiritual militia, employing an encoded language for truths that were to remain concealed from "the vulgar". This need for secrecy was urged by one of the most famous *Fedeli*, Francesco de Barberino (1264-1348), whilst another, Jacques de Baisieux, would say: "one must not reveal the counsels of love, but rather keep them carefully hidden". Scattered throughout Europe, the *Fedeli d'Amore* were linked with the troubadours and minstrels of the day, exalting the ideal of the Eternal Woman as associated with the supreme gift of the Holy Spirit (to which they referred as "Holy Love"). The veneration of Our Lady was their way of asserting the presence of the Paraclete (or "comforter") amongst the people with whom they settled. Royal courts were readily open to the *Fedeli*, themselves becoming "courts of love": this was famously true of the court of Alfonso X the Wise, king of Leon and Castille, and the court of Dinis I, the "troubadour" King of Portugal.

The *Fedeli* were not a heretical movement, but rather a group of free-thinking writers and artists who opposed the corruption of the Church and no longer recognised the popes as the spiritual head of Christendom. This opposition became keener after the bloody extermination of the Order of the Knights Templars by the king of France, Philip IV, and his "agent", Pope Clement V.

So, setting aside actual biographical details, the Beatrice of Dante's poem is, above all, a symbol of the Perfect Woman, of Divine Grace, and of the amorous soul that is a guarantee of spiritual immortality. Exemplifying the path of mystical purification, Beatrice represents that inner awakening which took place in Dante after his period of exile and his peregrinations in search of purification – peregrinations that finally came to an end when he re-discovered his immortal soul, symbolised by Beatrice.

CUBICLES OF THE TURKISH BATHS
IN THE HOTEL CASTELAR

1152 Avenida de Mayo
• Metro: line A, Lima station; line C, Avenida de Mayo station
• Visits to the baths can be arranged for those who are not guests of the hotel by calling + 54 11 4383-5000

Famous lockers

Ringo Bonavena, Aníbal Troilo (the football star of La Boca), Paulo Valentim, Sandro and Ricardo Balbin are all names inscribed deep down beneath Avenida de Mayo, where the city's oldest Turkish baths can be found. What do they have in common? They all enjoyed sweating out toxins into a white towel.

The place has kept the same lockers since it was opened almost a century ago. The Hotel Castelar was founded in 1929 and is famous for the celebrities, such as Federico Garcia Lorca (see p. 53) and Sandro, who have stayed there over the years. Sandro, for instance, was notorious among the sauna's staff for taking long-drawn-out afternoon naps there. He would smoke two whole packets of cigarettes in spite of the already steamy atmosphere, drink whisky and then fall asleep. Others, such as the radical politician Ricardo Balbin, came

here to tell the famous story of when he embraced Perón. "El Gordo" Troilo, the famous tango musician, was also a regular guest here. He used the same locker (the first from the left) twice a week and gave money to other guests to buy his records while he was there. You can still see the dent in the old refrigerator, in the entrance hall, made by Ringo Bonavena when he punched it in a rage one day, saying that he was not being served quickly enough.

There are many other, more or less well-known, names of regulars on plaques: Pascual Pérez, Edmundo Rivero, Tato Bores, Armando Bo, Javier Portales … all of whom left their mark on the history of the sauna's changing rooms. The stories have since become urban legends. Although some of the plaques have been stolen over the years, fans can still get changed in their favourite star's cubicles for free.

Although the place is not well known to the general public and the hotel does not offer guided tours, it does allow visitors (providing that they call beforehand) to go down and take photos, free of charge.

FEDERICO GARCÍA LORCA'S ROOM

Hotel Castelar
1100 Avenida de Mayo
• Guided tours: Wed 5pm–6.30 pm (20 pesos)

> **"Your arrival is a feast for the intelligence"**

I n October 1933 Frederico García Lorca, the famous Spanish poet and playwright, arrived in Argentina to present *Blood Wedding*. He stayed at the Hotel Castelar in room 704 on the seventh floor. It has been preserved ever since with its original iron bed. On the desk is one of Lorca's drawings and a personal diary where he kept notes on the Spanish Civil War. In this room he entertained his friends, the Argentinian poet Alfonsina Storni and the Chilean writer Pablo Neruda.

Lorca was invited to Buenos Aires by Lola Membrives, a famous Argentinian actress. He stayed longer than he had originally planned, leaving only at the beginning of 1934.

During this period, he dined with Oliverio Girondo, Carlos Gardel, Victoria Ocampo and many other illustrious names on Argentina's cultural scene. As a sign of their affection, these intellectuals sent him a telegram saying: "Your arrival is a feast for the intelligence."

"There is something intensely alive and unique about Buenos Aires, its heart beats fast … There is undoubtedly an air of nostalgia in Argentina that I cannot break away from." The poet wrote these lines in a room that he was never to see again: soon after he returned to Spain in 1936, he was arrested by Franco's militia and shot for his political views and sexual orientation.

In 2003 the Andalusian poet's hotel room was converted into a small museum and opened to the public. The hands of an alarm clock remain ominously stuck at 5 o'clock, the time at which the Spanish Civil War broke out.

Although the layout of the room that you can see today is not an exact replica, there are some interesting pictures of characters from Lorca's plays *The Shoemaker's Prodigious Wife* and *The House of Bernarda Alba* hanging in the corridor outside. On the seventh floor of the hotel, a display of photographs and short texts gives an insight into Lorca's life. Among these are his birth certificate and some handwritten letters, one of which was composed just before he left Buenos Aires. It shows his affection for the city: "Each street, each walk, evokes memories for me."

MUSEO DE INFORMÁTICA DE LA REPÚBLICA ㉙ ARGENTINA

810 Calle Tucuman
- Metro: line C, Esmeralda station; line D, 9 de Julio station; line B, Diagonal Norte station
- Tel: + 54 11 4393-3580
- www.museodeinformatica.org.ar

> *All the devices are in working order*

The Commodore 64 model is probably the first personal computer that Argentinians will remember. It was brought out in 1982, heralding the arrival of computers into people's homes, and it has pride of place in the Computer History Museum's collection of over 5,000 computers displayed in the basement of the building in Calle Tucuman.

Carlos Chiodini is the collector who supplied the museum with all manner of electronic devices from the last forty years. He set up the ICATEC (Information Technology, Computers and Technological Accessories) Foundation which now runs it. The museum was established in 2012, when Chiodini realised that he was running out of space at his home. It was the first of its kind in Argentina and the fifth in the world (see *Secret Madrid* by the same publisher).The devices on display include PCs, calculators, mobile phones and floppy disk players.

Perhaps the most surprising thing about the collection is that the devices are all in working order. This is thanks to the hard work of the museum staff, who ensure that they are restored and that the collection constantly evolves. A visit to this museum is the ideal way to appreciate just how far computer technology has come in such a short space of time. The legendary IBM 5150, the Apple Lisa (named by Steve Jobs after his daughter) and the Altair 8800 (one of the first computers used by Bill Gates) are some of the highlights of the collection.

Unlike the Computer History Museum in Mountain View, California, which is housed in an emblematic building belonging to Silicon Graphics,

ICATEC does not receive any external financial support despite the fact that it has been declared a Site of Cultural Interest by the city of Buenos Aires. It has therefore been forced to close some of its exhibition rooms and today the museum puts on thematic, mobile exhibitions in order to bring its impressive collection to the general public.

FRESCO BY BERNI IN GALERÍAS PACÍFICO 🄴

Avenida Cordoba and Calle Florida
• Metro: line C, Lavalle station; line B, Florida station

> *Love or the Germination of the Earth*

Although the frescoes in the main dome of the Galerías Pacífico shopping centre are a popular tourist attraction, very few people know that part of this "commercial Sistine Chapel" was designed by Antonio Berni (1905–1981). With his Modernist vision of 20th-century art, Berni was one of Argentina's most influential artists.

In 1946 five artists were commissioned to decorate the concrete central dome (450 m²) of the Galerías building, which was intended to become a reference for shopping centres throughout the world.

Juan Carlos Castagnino, Antonio Berni, Lino Enea Spilimbergo, Manuel Colmeiro and Demetrio Urruchua worked together to create a décor full of images from diverse cultures. Even if the works come together in a rather chaotic kind of collage, we can, nonetheless, distinguish the distinctive style of each artist.

Berni's fresco, *El Amor o Germinación de la Tierra* (Love or the Germination of the Earth), represents the union between Heaven and Earth. It shows a couple lying against a tree trunk, which represents the tangible world. This forms a contrast with the dreamlike, allegorical images of the immaterial world that are portrayed in the background.

For those who would like to take a closer look at this work, step into the building from Calle Florida and glance up to the right towards the centre of the dome.

EVA PERON'S RECEPTION ROOM

Palacio de la Legislatura
160 Calle Perú
• Metro: line A, Perú station; line E, Bolívar station
• Telephone bookings for guided tours: +54 11 4338-3000, ext. 1040/1041

*Inside
Evita's private
world*

I t is now possible to enter Evita's private world by visiting the Salón Eva Perón in the Legislative Palace: here you will be able to see her dressing table, her wardrobe and her three bathrooms in a suite that was very nearly forgotten. Her reception room, which is on the ground floor of the palace, behind the Salón Dorado (Golden Reception Room), is covered in hand-polished white marble and measures 60 m². In 2012 it was fully restored, with all its woodwork, wrought-iron features and drapes, and with the greatest attention to detail. The room also had a huge mirror that entirely covered one of its walls.

It is a little-known fact that the Eva Perón Foundation set up its headquarters here between 1946 and 1952. Consequently, Evita spent several hours a day here, using the same office that her husband had occupied from 1943 to 1945 when he was still the Secretary of Labour and Welfare and the ministry headquarters were there. We know for a fact that she received everyone who came to the foundation regardless of their needs and the nature of their requests for welfare benefits. On these occasions, Evita always made sure that she was immaculately dressed by using this small annex where she could change her clothes and renew her make-up as often as she liked.

The restoration project required a great deal of work as, during the 1955 Revolución Libertadora (Liberating Revolution) that overthrew Perón, the slightest evidence of his supporters was removed and only the small bronze plaque, indicating the whereabouts of the former office, was spared.

In addition to the main rooms, the restoration team worked on more neglected parts of the building, such as the toilets and some of the original furniture that had been left to rot. Using old photos, they managed to research and recreate the original layout.

JUAN DOMINGO AND EVA PERÓN'S WALKS TOGETHER UNDER THE PERGOLA

The Legislative Palace was used as the headquarters of the Eva Perón Foundation for several years between 1946 and 1952. At this time, Juan Perón was in his first term as president, and it is said that the general liked to take a break under the pergola on the terrace of the palace. This area, together with the gardens and the interior patio, has been fully restored and is now open to the public.

GUIDED TOUR OF THE LEGISLATURA CLOCK TOWER 🔢

160 Calle Perú
- Metro: line E, Bolívar station; line A, Perú station; line D, Catedral station
- Guided tours every day except Thurs
- Reservations: tel. +54 11 4338 3000, ext. 1040/1041, Mon–Fri 10am–6pm

Perón and Evita's customary stroll

The Legislatura (City Legislature) clock is one of the few monumental clocks still functioning in Buenos Aires. To find this gem of Argentinian architectural heritage, just follow the pigeons frightened away by its hourly chimes throughout the day.

The enormous clock is located at a height of 97 metres, at the top of the tower of the Palace of the Buenos Aires Legislatura, one of the highest towers in the old city. It has four dials, each measuring 4.5 metres in diameter. In 1931, when the building was opened, it was the largest clock in the world (a record that it kept for a year). Its carillon is still, however, highly impressive: manufactured in Berlin, it consists of about thirty bells weighing roughly 27 tonnes in total (the largest sounding G, and the smallest C) and a mechanical piano.

Surprising as it may seem, the tower and the clock were closed for many years and remained in a worrying state of neglect until early 2013, when a restoration campaign was launched.

Since that time, it has been possible to take guided tours of the building. The tower is reached via the stairway or the elevator. This leads to a room situated behind the clock dial, from which another staircase leads to the bell tower. It is known that Perón and his wife Evita would walk by this tower during their customary strolls.

The tour also includes entry to another unmissable secret location: Evita's dressing room (see preceding double-page spread).

ROVERANO ARCADE

506 Avenida de Mayo
• Metro: line A, Perú station; line D, Catedral station; line E, Bolívar station
• Buses: 2, 7, 24, 33, 50, 62, 86, 91, 105, 152

The Roverano Arcade is an unusual passageway, located on the ground floor of a 100-year-old building on Avenida de Mayo next to the Cabildo, which has the distinction of being the only building in the city with its own direct access to the metro system.

> *The city's only building with its own metro entrance*

The arcade bears the name of its founders, and owners, brothers Ángel and Pascual Roverano, the sons of Italian immigrants who had come to make their fortune in the Americas. In 1878 these ambitious merchants commissioned a luxury office building that still embodies the style of the period: huge windows, marble columns and original woodwork. Immediately next door is a hair salon dating from the same period that, until recently, used to count Cardinal Jorge Bergoglio (now Pope Francis) as one of its clients.

In 1888, during the initial phases of construction work on the Avenida de Mayo, some buildings were destroyed or altered to make way for the new road layout. The Roverano Arcade was one of the buildings affected by these changes. By way of compensation, the Buenos Aires authorities granted it a small privilege in 1915: permission to establish direct and exclusive access to line A of the new underground railway. As a result, Perú station can be reached from any floor, without ever leaving the building, simply by taking the elevator.

Although the arcade is private property, its commercial section is open to the public, which means that visitors can satisfy their curiosity merely by taking the corridor that leads down into the depths of the city.

STORIES FROM THE ARCADE

The Roverano Arcade has given birth to a number of stories. During the early 1930s, Antoine de Saint-Exupéry, author of *The Little Prince*, was for a time a familiar face in the building's corridors while working for Aeroposta Argentina, whose office was situated on the second floor. He visited regularly to collect the mail sacks that he transported from the capital city to Patagonia.

Another office was the scene of a historic meeting in 1970 between Ricardo Balbín and one of Perón's representatives. The meeting in question was the first to be held between radicals and Peronists for the purposes of defining what would later be called the *"Hora del Pueblo"* (Hour of the People), an alliance that led to the end of the military dictatorship that had removed President Illia.

EGYPTIAN PYRAMIDS IN THE METROPOLITAN ㉔ CATHEDRAL

437 Avenida Rivadavia
• Metro: line A, Perú station; line D, Bolívar station

When visiting the Metropolitan Cathedral for the first time, visitors are genuinely surprised to see Egyptian pyramids on the tympanum on the façade of the building. The scene depicts the moment when the Hebrew patriarch Joseph was reunited with his father Jacob and his eleven brothers, representing the twelve tribes of Israel. According to the Holy Gospel, this meeting took place at the Pharaoh's court and the pyramids of Giza are there to illustrate this.

> *The place where Joseph the patriarch, his father Jacob and his eleven brothers were reunited*

Rumour has it that the bas-relief was sculpted in 1863 by a prisoner who was pardoned after he completed the work. In reality, it is by the French sculptor Joseph Dubourdieu, who also made the Statue of Liberty that stands on the Pyrámide de Mayo (in the Plaza de Mayo).

During the same period, and as one of the consequences of the battle of Pavon (1861), the Province of Buenos Aires was reunited with the rest of the country: there is a link between this reconciliation and the scene of reunion represented on the tympanum of the cathedral.

THE FAÇADE OF THE METROPOLITAN CATHEDRAL IS NOT A COPY OF LA MADELEINE IN PARIS

It has often been said that the façade of the Metropolitan Cathedral is a copy of La Madeleine in Paris. In reality, the only thing they have in common is that they were both built in a neoclassical style. The cathedral in Buenos Aires was built in 1822 whereas La Madeleine in Paris dates from 1842.

FORMER CONGRESS OF THE NATION

139 Calle Balcarce
• Metro: line A, Plaza de Mayo station; line D, Catedral station; line E, Bolívar station
• Visits: Thurs–Fri 3pm–5pm

A historical site hidden in the AFIP building

It is a little-known fact that until the end of the 19th century, the seat of the first Legislative Palace was situated a few metres from the Casa Rosada on Calle Balcarce.

Some of the old features of the former Congress can still be seen today in the AFIP (Federal Administration of Inland Revenue), the equivalent of the British HMRC (Her Majesty's Revenue and Customs).

The building's conservation is now in the hands of the National Academy of History, as it has been declared a national Historical Monument.

The former Congress was located there from 1864 until 1905, when it had to move, as it lacked sufficient seating for all the Congressmen – a consequence of the growth in the city's population towards the end of the 19th century. The building was almost entirely demolished, except for the main reception room, the galleries, the lodges, its peristyle and its entrance gate.

Some of the original items, including furniture such as the stenographers' table, the benches and an enormous portrait of an illustrious member of parliament, Valentine Alsina (1802–1869), have been restored and are now on display.

Visitors can also see a collection of manuscripts, documents, pictures and newspapers covering forty-one years of the sessions held here by the two chambers of Congress.

It is therefore possible to dip into records of memorable debates such as those that led to the declaration of war against Uruguay or a vote on immigration laws, all in the words of Argentina's greatest politicians.

If you take a closer look, you may even see Sarmiento's famous phrase, which is often quoted in the history books: "My fists are full of truth."

SIGNS OF DAMAGE LEFT BY THE BOMBING

Ministry of Finance, Hacienda Palace
100 Paseo Colón
• Metro: line A, Plaza de Mayo station

> *Souvenirs of an attempted coup d'état*

Buenos Aires has discreet, yet permanent, scars that have become an integral part of its landscape. On 16 June 1955 aircraft from the Argentine Navy and Air Force strafed and bombed the Plaza de Mayo and the Casa Rosada during an attempted coup d'état to overthrow General Peron's government. An eyewitness is quoted as saying: "When we arrived in the area, one of the last planes swooped over us, guns blazing. We took shelter in the Ministry of Finance building. The bullet holes remained there for many years. I don't know if they can still be seen there."

They are, in fact, still visible today: the small dents in the marble are not due to erosion or to the passing of time. They are the scars from a dark page of Argentina's history and can be seen on the front of the Hacienda Palace, on the southern side of the Plaza de Mayo, along the Avenida Paseo Colón.

Many of the bullet holes left by heavy artillery fire were still visible on the building in the 1990s until Carlos Menem's government had it restored. Today, however, the remaining bullet holes and a commemorative plaque testify to this dramatic event in Argentina's history.

It is thought that 10 tonnes of bombs were dropped on Buenos Aires during the bombing of the city, killing 308 people and injuring 700, most of whom were civilians in or around the square at the time.

This bombing was a forewarning of the coup d'état that took place three months later, leading to the overthrow of President Peron by the Liberating Revolution.

Tragically, this kind of atrocity has not been uncommon in Argentina's history. The first was perpetrated during the British invasions in 1806 and 1807 and was followed closely by a similar event at the battle of Los Pozos in 1811. The third occurred during the self-declared Park Revolution, a fascist civilian and military uprising that came to a head on 26 June 1890.

On the night of 16 June 1955, as an act of revenge after the Plaza de Mayo bombing, Peronist supporters set fire to the San Francisco and Santo Domingo cathedrals as well as churches situated in the wealthier areas of the city.

SAN TELMO
AND SURROUNDINGS

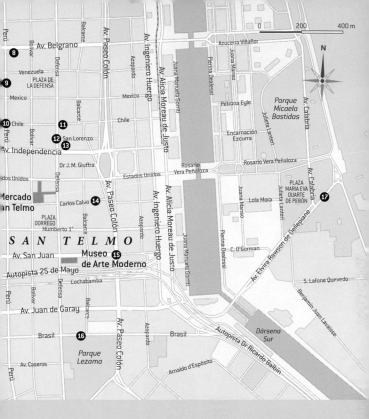

TODO SE OLVIDA
CON EL CHAMPAGNE

LA BOTICA DEL ÁNGEL

543 Avenida Luis Sáenz Peña, Congreso district
• Metro: line A, Sáenz Peña station; line C, Moreno station; line E, Lima station
• Guided tours: Wed and Fri 7pm
• Information and bookings on 0800 333 8725

A psychedelic museum with one of the city's most iconoclastic artistic heritage collections

The Angel's Pharmacy is a wonderful cultural hotchpotch. The visitor will find works by Juan Carlos Castagnino rubbing shoulders with works by Raul Soldi, Guillermo Roux, Marta Minujin (among others), texts written by Manual Mujica Láinez, Jorge Luis Borges, Alejandra Pizarnik and Ernesto Sabato, in addition to souvenirs of Carlos Gardel and various film posters. The museum's café is decorated in the same spirit, with objects from some of the famous old bars that make up Buenos Aires' past.

This museum-theatre was set up by Eduardo Bergara Leumann, an actor and emblematic figure of the 1960s and '70s in Argentina, and it has the city's most iconoclastic and impressive artistic heritage collection.

On 8 December 1966, during the "democratisation of culture" period, Leumann opened La Botica del Ángel where he lived at No. 670 on Calle Lima. The eccentric artist's home soon became a place where all sorts of events were organised, from shows to weird and wonderful exhibitions and heated cultural debates. All manner of artists, whether emerging, classical or modern, used La Botica before Avenida 9 de Julio was widened and the venue had to move to another site. It finally closed in 1973.

Four years later, Leumann decided to create a museum called La Botica del Ángel in an old building situated at No. 541 on Calle Luis Sáenz Peña in the Congreso district. The place was lovingly decorated and at the entrance visitors can read the following inscription: "Here you will find everything that you thought was lost."

Leumann, the creator of this "museum-house of art" died on 5 September 2008 at the age of 76.

A MONUMENT TO BRIBES

Building of the former Ministry of Public Works
1925 Avenida 9 de Julio
• Metro: line C, Moreno station; line E, Belgrano station

> **She holds out her hand while looking away**

A t the corners of the front of the former Ministry of Public Works building, which is now home to the Ministries of Health and Social Development and which looks out on to Avenida 9 de Julio and Calle Moreno, there are two statues which are almost swallowed up by the huge Art Deco structure.

It is hard to make them out: located at either end of the second floor, they have complementary features. One of them carries a small box whereas the other puts a hand behind her back with her arm close to her side and gazes away, as if to accept the box. This is why the two statues are considered to be a monument to corruption.

The unofficial story goes that they were designed by the building's architect, José Hortal. He also drew up the project for the "first skyscraper funded by the State" in the 1930s and which was finally erected on the city's most important avenue (this is why it is a building with only one street number). It is said that Hortal – who was, at the time, the director of National Architecture – was so fed up with being offered bribes to finish the building more quickly that he put the statues up at the very last minute to denounce the fact that he had been subjected to so much corruption.

Although this was never publicly denied, it is nevertheless surprising that such a monument – denouncing corruption as it does from a public building – has managed to remain intact over the years.

PORTRAITS OF EVITA: THE SAME TECHNIQUE AS USED FOR CHE GUEVARA IN HAVANA

The two portraits of Eva Peron, which cover a large part of the north- and south-facing sides of the former Ministry of Public Works building, represent the public and political faces of Evita. They are 31 metres high and 24 metres wide and each one is made up of 42 steel parts, weighing a total of 14 tonnes. The work was executed by the Argentinian artist Alejandro Marmo and was inaugurated on 26 July 2011 for the 59th anniversary of the death of Evita (who had been nominated "Woman of the Bicentenary" a year earlier). Marmo used a similar technique to that adopted for the famous Che Guevara relief which stands outside the Cuban Ministry of the Interior, opposite Plaza de la Revolución.

MUSEO NACIONAL DE LA HISTORIA DEL TRAJE ❸

832 Calle Chile, San Telmo district
• Metro: lines C and E, Independencia station
• Open Tues–Sun, 3pm–7pm. Free admission
• Guided tours available: advance booking essential on
+ 54 11 4343-8427

I t is hard to understand why the National
Museum of Costume History has not been
more successful. There are more than
8,000 pieces on display and the collection is
regularly renewed and updated.

Four centuries of history seen through clothes

The museum is located in one of the typical
chorizo houses that were built at the end of the 19th century. It is one of the few
houses of its kind that is still intact: the mouldings, the gates, the woodwork
and the marble skirting boards that decorate the entrance hall are all original
features.

More importantly, inside the museum, visitors can see an impressive
collection of costumes and accessories retracing the history of Argentina from
the 18th century to the present day.

At whatever time of year you decide to visit, there will be different
exhibitions such as "The Swinging Twenties" (when women shortened their
skirts up to the knee); swimming costumes from 1890 to the present day;
reproductions of Harrods' famous window displays from the 1950s; or an
intriguing collection of shoes, with a pair of Chinese "lotus feet" dating back to
the 10th century. These shoes caused terrible suffering by forcing young girls
to squeeze their feet into them to respect the ancestral traditions imposed by
their social rank.

"The Truth about Fashion in 1810" is also worth a visit. The myth
surrounding women at the time of the May Revolution is taken apart and
commonly believed facts are shown to be untrue. The beauties of that period
did not wear extravagant combs in their hair, nor did they dress in crinolines.
Women's colonial fashion at that time meant a slim figure, tightly pulled in
at the waist with a corset, a tubular skirt and short puffed sleeves. In reality,
women looked much more like Snow White than those traditionally portrayed
at these patriotic demonstrations.

Once or twice a year, the museum holds the "Night of the Phantoms": the
tour starts at twilight and visitors get to see places that are not usually
open to the public.

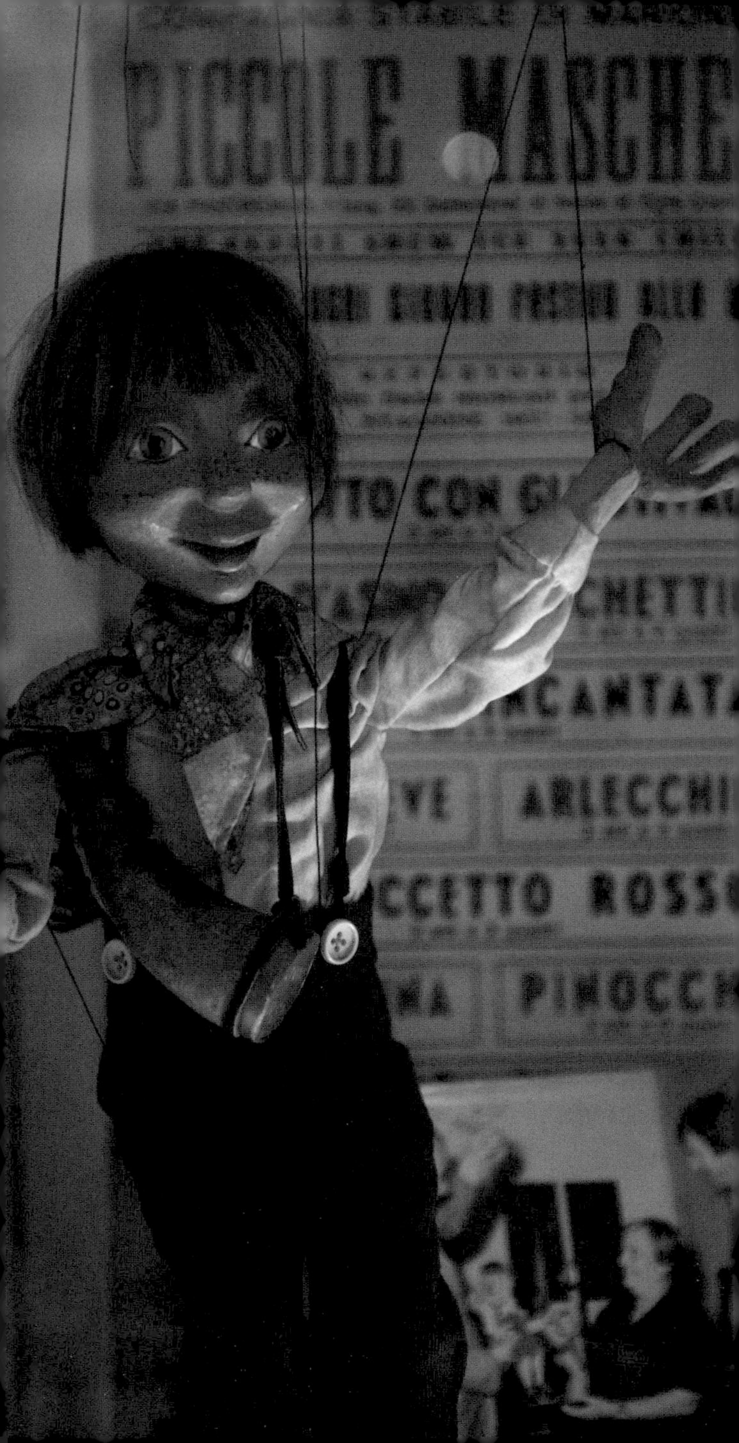
PICCOLE

MUSEO ARGENTINO DEL TÍTERE ❹

905 Piedras, San Telmo district
• Metro: lines C and E, Independencia station
• Open Wed–Sun 3pm–6pm
• Puppet shows for children on Sat and Sun 4.30pm

> *A collection of 600 puppets*

Although puppetry is an ancient art, there is only one museum dedicated to it in the whole of Argentina: in 1983, with the help of Mane Bernardo and Sarah Bianchi, two employees of the national puppet-making workshop, the Argentine Puppetry Museum was set up. It now has a collection of around 600 different models of puppets on display, classified according to their origin and the techniques used to make them.

The building housing the San Telmo museum was constructed in the early 20th century by Mane Bernardo's family and it was gradually transformed over the years from their family home into a museum. In the early days, the Bernardos had a travelling puppet show, giving more than fifty performances throughout the country, but as time went on, their puppet collection grew and the place became a permanent museum. The late Sarah Bianchi spent much of her life raising funds to finance the museum and its development.

The puppets on display range from local to foreign and from traditional techniques, such as glove puppets, to the more modern models which use a thimble or a stick. There is a special exhibition dedicated to the famous La Plata puppeteer, Carlos Moneo Sanz, with puppets from television shows or seen in advertising (there is even a puppet used by Federico Garcia Lorca during a show in Buenos Aires). In a rather cramped room at the heart of the Latin American collection, La Lola and Mireya Cueto represent two famous Mexican actors. Some puppets are over a hundred years old; they are so fragile that they look as if they could crumble into dust at any moment.

SANTA CASA DE EJERCICIOS ESPIRITUALES ❺
SOR MARÍA ANTONIA DE LA PAZ Y FIGUEROA

1190 Avenida Independencia
- Metro: lines C and E, Independencia station
- Open on the first Sunday of the month (request times)
- Spiritual retreats on request
- Information: + 54 11 4304-0984/4305-4618

> **All the most powerful people of the time visited the convent**

The Sor Maria Antonia de la Paz y Figueroa Sacred House of Spiritual Exercises was built in 1795 and is probably one of the best examples of colonial architecture in Buenos Aires. It is still in use today and the main part of its original structure has been preserved.

The main wall was built of rammed earth and the wooden gate which opens out onto Avenida Independencia is an important relic. It leads to a place where time has stood still and has all its original features, such as the floors, openings, furniture and decoration from the 1880s.

The house was founded by María Antonia de la Paz y Figueroa (from Santiago del Estero) and became the first school for girls and a home for young girls who had been abandoned. It was also used as a retreat for an endless list of celebrities such as Cornelio Saavedra, Jacques de Liniers, Manuel Belgrano, Mariano Moreno, Bernardino Rivadavia, Juan José Castelli, Juan Bautista Alberdi and Juan Manuel de Rosas.

The building has been declared a National Historical Monument as it is a valuable part of the city's heritage.

It can only be visited on the second Sunday of the month as it is still used as a spiritual retreat. If you are lucky enough to visit, you will be able to walk

through its colonial patios and its cloisters and see the nuns' cells and the chapels, which are full of superb examples of Baroque Jesuit art. There is a striking picture of Jesus Christ from Cuzco in one of the chapels, which is dedicated to Jesus of Nazareth.

Another room has a cross made of carob wood, weighing an impressive 45 kg. Penitents had to carry these crosses on their shoulders and one can be still found hanging on the cloister wall.

A REHABILITATION CENTRE FOR UNRULY WOMEN

From the end of the 18th century up to the beginning of the 19th, the Sor Maria Antonia de la Paz y Figueroa Sacred House of Spiritual Exercises was also used as a place to "save" women at a time when they had very few rights. Women who were awaiting trial or who did not have a male guardian were also "confined" here.

"Marquita Sanchez was confined here for disobeying her parents" is written on one of the plaques on a bedroom door.

The 15-year-old was punished for the relationship she was having with her cousin, Martin Thompson. She did, however, manage to marry him in the end, despite her parents' disapproval.

Camilla O'Gorman was another unfortunate young woman who stayed here: she was arrested with a priest called Ladislao Gutierrez while they were preparing to elope to another country – she was brought back to Buenos Aires.

Thanks to her friend Manuelita de Rosas, the daughter of the governor of Buenos Aires, she was transferred to the convent to await trial. She even managed to obtain a room with a grand piano (on display in the Americas Room) but, tragically, Juan Manuel de Rosas refused to release the young woman and ordered her execution: Camilla, who was eight months pregnant, was shot by firing squad on 18 August 1848.

DECORATED DOOR OF THE BIBLIOTECA DEL DOCENTE

⑥

1349 Avenida Entre Rios
• Open Mon–Fri 9am–6pm
• Metro: line E, Entre Rios-Rodolfo Walsh station
• Buses: 4, 12, 37, 84, 96, 168, 195

A door inspired by the Baptistery in Florence?

For eighty years the door of the del Docente Library, at No. 1300 Avenida Entre Rios, led through to the Carlos Pellegrini Complex, consisting of two schools and a public library.

This monument in the form of a door shows (in only a few square metres) the history of education in Argentina: it was sculpted by Arturo Dresco (1875–1961) as a tribute to teachers and was inaugurated on 11 September 1933.*

The work comprises eight bronze panels, with reliefs showing landscapes from the country's various regions: each panel shows the typical tasks of the teacher and stresses the sacrifice made by those who had to teach in remote rural and border areas.

On the sides of this imposing, 3 metre-high structure are several political figures who contributed to the development of the Argentinian education system: Sarmiento, Rivadavia, Belgrano and Moreno.

The work also shows the local flora and fauna in addition to the shields of the fourteen provinces that once made up the Republic of Argentina.

The door has many similar features to a Renaissance masterpiece in Florence: the doors of the Baptistery of St John the Baptist (known as the "Gates of Paradise").

It is highly likely that Dresco was inspired by this work of art as he finished his training as a sculptor in Florence.

Although this historic door was used as an entrance to the library for many years, time took its toll and in 2013 the city council took it away for restoration. It can now be seen in the hall of the library.

*11 September is Pan-American Teachers' Day: it commemorates the death of Domingo Faustino Sarmiento, considered to be the father of State education in Argentina.

GHOSTS OF PASAJE MOMPOX

1600 Pasaje Mompox, Barracas district
• Metro: line E, Entre-Rios-Rodolfo Walsh station

> *Only
> the blood
> of the defeated
> shall remain*

In the Barracas area, north of the city centre, there is a notoriously mysterious passage called Pasaje Mompox.

In March 1978, at the crossroads of Calles Mompox and Garay, Sergio, a student who worked part-time in a friend's grocery, was kidnapped and held hostage by a group of soldiers. In the 1990s, the neighbours said that one day they had heard a young man shouting for help in the closed-up shop. Was this true or was the story invented to draw people's attention to the hard social reality of the time and to help the plight of the Mothers of the Plaza de Mayo?

Five blocks down from Plaza de la Constitución, at No. 1636 in Calle Mompox, a gate leads to the corridor of an old *chorizo* house. At the back of the house is a staircase. People say that, on some nights, a dim light can be seen shining from the roof and that they can hear the blades of two daggers clashing like church bells. It is thought that this story comes from a duel between two local villains, in a fight to see who would take over the area.

However, no one won the duel and all that was left of the two opponents was the blood they had shed. Ever since this fateful evening, and often during a full moon, the silence of the night is broken by a mysterious clashing noise. It would be true to say there are fewer residents living in this lane than the number of stories that have been told about it.

frío polar
en su hogar

HELADERAS **Polaris**

BANHAM Hnos. y Cía.   PERÚ 362

ADVERTISEMENT FOR POLARIS REFRIGERATORS

8

Avenida Belgrano 600
• Metro line E, Belgrano station; line A, Perú station
• Bus 2, 7, 22, 74, 86, 91

> **An advertisement dating from 1939**

I n the Montserrat neighbourhood, at the intersection of Calle Perú and Avenida Belgrano, there is an old advertisement extolling the merits of "Polaris" refrigerators.

It depicts a well-stocked white refrigerator connected to the North Pole, supplying it with polar cold. This original idea was thought up by the great Lino Palacio (1903-1984), a designer, script writer, painter and graphic and commercial artist. At the bottom of the mural, the address "Perú 362" is indicated as belonging to the business owned by the Banham brothers, which sold the refrigerator, and its telephone number. Nothing remains of their store today.

The reason for the survival of the advertisement remains a mystery. In September 2007, it was declared part of the "cultural heritage of the city of Buenos Aires" after detailed restoration undertaken in 1990 with support from the Secretariat of Culture and an art school, whose students and teachers restored the mural to its original clarity.

Standing on the other side of the "patio porteño" (a term used to describe the area at the corner of the street that has not been built on), it is still possible to read the old tagline: "Polaris refrigerators: cold from the Pole in your home".

STATUE OF *THE BLACKSMITH* 　　　　　**9**

Club Museum San Telmo
535 Calle Peru, Monserrat district
• Metro: line E, Belgrano station
• Buses: 22, 64, 86, 130, 152
• Open at weekends in the evening

The Club Museum is situated in the Monserrat area and is famous for having been designed by Gustave Eiffel. The columns and capitals of the building were shipped over from France in 1906 and assembled on site by a local architect in Buenos Aires.

A souvenir of Eiffel's windmill-making workshop

It took over ten years to build it in a typically French style and the building was finally inaugurated as an agricultural tool- and windmill-making workshop. Originally called *The Blacksmith,* it still has a statue on top of the front of the building and has been declared a Historic Monument.

The statue, which was created by the Argentinian architect Lorenzo Siegaris, is the only original feature that remains as a reminder of the building's past. The enormous hangar has been converted into what is now a popular discotheque. The basement, the ground floor and the two other floors, all built of steel, are now used as VIP lounges, restaurants and bars.

Before it became the Club Museum, the building (which dates back to 1757) was used as a luxury residence by Vicente Lopez y Planes (the composer of the Argentinian National Anthem) and had magnificent gardens. Another of Eiffel's creations stands in the Province of Cordoba, in Capilla del Monte. This is where the famous engineer built a windmill when he entered a competition organised by the Argentine Agricultural Show.

THE BALCONY OF RODOLFO WALSH

Intersection of Avenida Chile and Calle Perú, San Telmo
• Metro line E, Belgrano station; line C, Independencia station

> **The memory of a writer who was a victim of the last military dictatorship**

On the small square located at the intersection of Avenida Chile and Calle Perú, several benches, a withered shrub and some ineffective street lamps create an atmosphere worthy of a detective story. One of the walls, which is covered with sketches and quotations by Rodolfo Walsh (1927-1977), serves as a reminder of the assassination of this writer, journalist and author of *Operation Massacre* (see box below).

Walsh was gunned down on 25 March 1977 on the corner of Avenida San Juan and Avenida Entre Ríos after his famous *Open Letter from a Writer to the Military Junta*, which attacked the economic devastation wrought by the dictatorship of the Argentine generals, had been made public.

At the back of the square bearing his name, a statue of Walsh stands on a fake balcony, surrounded by the titles of his works and their years of publication. The illustrations associated with the figure are completed by a typewriter, a cup of black coffee and thick glasses. The mural was created by artists from the HIJOS group (the acronym for *Hijos e Hijas por la Identidad y la Justicia contra el Olvido y el Silencio*, "Sons and Daughters for Identity and Justice Against Oblivion and Silence", an Argentinian human rights organisation).

The "little square", as it is known locally, was restored on the initiative of the Buenos Aires Secretariat of Culture in 2009; the project involved repairing the wall decorated by the members of HIJOS.

Rodolfo Walsh Plaza, a symbolic site of commemoration dedicated to the men and women who have made their mark on the history of Buenos Aires, also displays several plaques paying tribute to the inhabitants of San Telmo who disappeared during the last dictatorship.

THE "HOUSE" OF MAFALDA ⑪

371 Calle Chile, San Telmo district
• Metro: line E, Belgrano station
• Buses: 8, 22, 29, 86, 103, 195

> **Quino's character was born in this building in 1963**

One of the attractions in San Telmo is known as the "comic-strip promenade" (*el Paseo de la Historieta*), in reference to the statues depicting the most popular cartoon characters scattered throughout the streets. They include that of the famous Mafalda, located at the junction of Calle Defensa and Calle Chile. The sculpture, by Pablo Irrgang, shows the little girl seated on a bench, flanked by two of her friends, Susanita and Manolito. What is less well known, however, is that a few metres away, at No. 371, Calle Chile, is the "house" of Mafalda. The cartoonist Joaquín Lavado, known as Quino, lived for many years in an apartment in the building, and it was here that his pencil gave birth to his most famous character.

Although Mafalda was created in 1963, the first comic strip was not published until the end of 1964, in the mythical magazine *Primera Plana*. From 1965 Mafalda's adventures featured in the newspaper *El Mundo* and in 1967, when the latter ceased publication, the little girl's incisive and acerbic observations appeared in the weekly, *Siete Días*. Mafalda continued for ten years until the cartoon strip was published for the last time on 25 June 1973.

The idea of dedicating a statue to the child who asked awkward questions began to take root in 2005, when Caloi (creator of the comic-strip character Clemente) made a written request to the then mayor of the city, Aníbal Ibarra, for the house in San Telmo to be declared part of the city's urban

heritage. At the same time, Quino was recognised as an "illustrious citizen of the City of Buenos Aires". The petition ended with the words: "As citizens of the world and readers of this cartoon strip, we request that a commemorative plaque be installed on the front of the house where Mafalda lived prior to 31 December 2005." At the bottom were thousands of signatures in support of the project. Since then, passers-by have been able to see a plaque fixed to the door of the building, announcing: "*Aquí nació Mafalda*" (Mafalda was born here).

STATUE OF CARLITOS BALÁ

The Chacarita area pays homage to one of the greatest Argentinian comics, Carlitos Balá. His statue is found in Imperio, a pizzeria now classified as a site of cultural importance, and which has been in business since 1930. The history of the statue, which is impressively realistic, dates back to the 1950s, when Balá, who was about 20 years old, wandered the streets making jokes. He lived close to the terminus of the No. 39 bus and befriended the drivers, who allowed him on board their vehicles so that he could perform his first improvised sketches.

Balá recalls that these buses were his "school". At that time, and before he became a celebrity, the actor would end his improvised sketches by eating a slice of pizza at Imperio. In 2010 a statue was erected in his honour: you can see it if you enter through the door leading from Avenida Federico Lacroze.

EL ZANJÓN DE GRANADOS

755 Calle Defensa, San Telmo district
• Metro: line C, Independencia station
• Buses: 8, 22, 24, 29, 86
• Guided tours: Sun—Fri. Times on + 54 11 4361-3002

> *The first foundations of Buenos Aires*

The modern house standing between Calles Defensa, Chile and Balcarce and Avenida Independencia is the starting point of a maze of 400-year-old tunnels through which a stream of dirty water, known as El Zanjón de Granados, flowed before merging with the Rio de la Plata. Some historians say that this was where Pedro de Mendoza laid the city's first foundations in 1536.

As the city began to grow at the beginning of the 19th century, successive building sites buried these relics of the past. In 1985 a rather dilapidated house at 755 Calle Defensa changed hands for next to nothing. The tunnels were uncovered during the renovation work: this led to an archaeological dig on site for the next twenty years, aiming to retrace the city's history. This work was funded by the owners of the house, which later gained Cultural Heritage status.

Among the ruins, archaeologists found foundations, the remains of a wall, floors, earthenware, water tanks, utensils and documents dating back to various periods, all of which are on display in the El Zanjón Museum. The tunnels have been renovated and they now join up. For example, you can walk between the building on Calle Chili and the one on Calle Defensa through an underground tunnel.

Today, the place has been converted into an exhibition centre and events venue. Guided tours are available.

THE TINY HOUSE

380 Pasaje San Lorenzo, San Telmo district
• Buses: 8, 86, 130, 152, 195

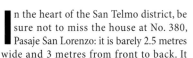

I n the heart of the San Telmo district, be sure not to miss the house at No. 380, Pasaje San Lorenzo: it is barely 2.5 metres wide and 3 metres from front to back. It looks like a dolls' house with an unassuming façade, peeping out between two other houses. Look out for its small Andalusian-style balcony with a moulded corniche.

The door to Hell

It is thought that the property was built in 1813, date of the Assembly of the Year XIII (a congress of deputies from the United Provinces of La Plata), held at a time when slavery had not been abolished. This point is significant as the first person who lived here is said to be the first black person to have been emancipated.

In the 1960s the house belonged to an antiques dealer who spread a frightening rumour that behind the tiny façade lay one of the seven doors of Hell.

The anthropologist Marcelo Pisarro gives us a much more rational explanation, suggesting that the house is no more than a real-estate curiosity: it originally formed part of the adjoining building at No. 392, which had an entrance on Calle Defensa. This property was knocked down in around 1840 and the ground was levelled to allow the construction of a wealthy family's large house with a double patio.

When this family finally moved out, the building was divided up into several lots for lease. In 1906 the façade was renovated and in the 20th century the property was split further between fifteen different owners. It therefore became smaller and smaller as the different lots were sold. If we are to believe Pisarro, the minuteness of the house is simply the result of a succession of real-estate deals.

TRAINING SHIP OF THE DANISH CHURCH

Dansk Kirke
257 Calle Carlos Calvo, San Telmo district
• Metro: line C, Independencia station
• Buses: 8, 33, 74, 86, 130, 152
• Advance booking essential on + 54 11 4362-9154. Admission free

*In memory
of the shipwreck*

The Danish church standing at No. 257 on Calle Carlos Calvo, in the heart of San Telmo, commemorates the greatest tragedy ever to hit the Danish community in Argentina. A model of the ship which sank in the 1920s can be seen today, hanging from the ceiling of the church, opposite the altar.

Kopenhavn (The Copenhagen), a training ship, set sail for Australia from Buenos Aires in July 1928 with many young Danish sailors from wealthy families on board. The ship, however, was only to sail 1,500 miles (about 2,400 km) before disappearing without a trace. It is a mystery as to why it sank and the shipwreck has never been found.

The church was inaugurated three years after the tragedy occurred with funds from the Danish community in Buenos Aires. It was built in an area near the harbour so that relatives of the unfortunate sailors could go there to pray. The building is in a neo-Gothic style, which makes it rather austere. Its exposed brick walls were built like a staircase to represent the staircase going up to the heavens that Jacob saw in his dream during his flight from his brother Esau.

It is not generally known in the area that there is a church in this dark, fenced off-place, as the shutters are often closed and there is no sign. The only hint that it is a church is its spire topped with a cross.

REMAINS OF THE SECRET DETENTION CENTRE, THE ATLÉTICO CLUB

15

1200 Avenida Paseo Colón
• Buses: 4, 8, 33, 64, 130, 152, 195

> *In memory of those who went missing during the last dictatorship*

Just in front of No. 1200 Avenida Paseo Colón, you will see the outline of a huge human figure. It is on the central reservation, under the motorway, at the intersection of Avenida Paseo Colón and Cochabamba and is a tribute to those who went missing during the last dictatorship. Many people were tortured in the secret detention centre that used to stand here – it was cynically called the "Atlético Club" due to the existence of the neighbouring Boca Juniors Club.

The ruins, where parts of the old cell walls can still be seen today, stand as a witness to past horrors. It is thought that as many as 1,800 people "went missing" here in under two years (the centre operated from mid-1976 to December 1977).

The centre was demolished to make way for a motorway and it remained buried for twenty-five years. Then, in April 2002, a group of archaeologists decided to start excavating the site to find the remains and to conserve the memory in the public mind. The digging work, which went down to 4 metres, uncovered the remains of cell walls with inscriptions on them, police uniforms, boots and even a rosary.

The project entailed a great deal of archaeological research and documentation. However, the valuable information provided by survivors of this centre undoubtedly made the greatest contribution and helped the archaeologists to know where to dig during the excavation process. In a book entitled *Nunca Más* (Never Again), one of these survivors is quoted as saying: "The basement of the Atlético was composed of two isolation cells, a torture chamber and an infirmary. There was no ventilation, no source of daylight and the place was very damp. In summer, the temperature went over 40°C, and in winter it was freezing cold."

The central reservation has since been declared a Historical Monument by the city council.

CATEDRAL ORTODOXA RUSA DE LA SANTÍSIMA TRINIDAD

315 Avenida Brasil
• Buses: 10, 24, 33, 62, 64, 86, 93, 129, 152, 159
• Visits: second Sunday of the month at 3 pm
• Mass: Sunday 10 am

Slavic liturgy and Gregorian chants

Be careful not to miss the only Russian Orthodox church in Buenos Aires as it is tucked away among the buildings on Avenida Brasil: the Cathedral of the Most Holy Trinity is a piece of Moscow in the heart of San Telmo. Those who stand just opposite, in Parque Lezama, will be able to admire the building's wonderfully exotic architectural beauty from a different angle.

Visitors will, of course, be dazzled by the bulb-shaped, bright turquoise bell towers (covered in shiny gold stars representing the Virgin Mary) and the building's magnificent pediment, but they must take time to step inside.

The layout of Orthodox churches comes from a thousand-year-old tradition dating back to the construction of the Lord's first home by Moses, 1,500 years BC. The liturgy is composed of various holy accessories such as the altar, the seven-branched candelabra, the incense and the priestly robes. During the services there is no organ playing and microphones are not used as the Orthodox Church believes that only the human voice can reach God.

Much as New York Gospel choirs attract tourists to Harlem, a visit to this Orthodox cathedral, with its traditional services and Gregorian chants in the Slavic languages, takes visitors outside the more conventional tourist circuits.

Visitors are welcome as long as they abide by the following rules: women must cover their heads and wear long skirts during services. No lipstick must be worn, to avoid leaving marks after kissing the icons, the cross and the chalice. During the service everyone, except for the elderly, must remain standing. Neither visits nor questions are allowed during the service, as this could disturb those who are praying. Leaving the church before the end of the service is considered an offence. It is forbidden to take photos in the cathedral.

MUSEO DE CALCOS Y ESCULTURA COMPARADA "ERNESTO DE LA CÁRCOVA"

1701 Avenida España
• Open Tues–Sun. 1 April–31 Oct: 10am– 6pm. 1 Nov–31 March:
11am–7pm
• Buses: 2, 4, 20, 64, 103, 111, 130, 152

> **South America's most important sculptural heritage**

The Ernesto de la Cárcova Museum of Reproductions and Comparative Sculpture is situated close to the Ecological Reserve. It has on display the most important sculptural heritage of South America: the most significant replicas of the world's sculptures are held here.

The sight of the copy of Michelangelo's *David* is sure to take your breath away as you start the visit. This plaster replica is extraordinarily like the real statue, with remarkable attention to detail: every muscle and expression have been painstakingly reproduced to express the sheer beauty and perfection of the human body.

The real value of the museum's collections lies in the quality of its 700 reproductions. Among the more remarkable pieces on display are the *Pietà* and *Moses,* both works by Michelangelo; the *Venus de Milo*; the head of the Egyptian Queen Nefertiti; and the *Winged Victory of Samothrace.* There are also collections devoted to reproductions of masterpieces from Egyptian, Chaldean, Graeco-Roman, medieval and oriental art. All the reproductions are to scale and are exact copies of the originals as they were moulded or cast in original moulds.

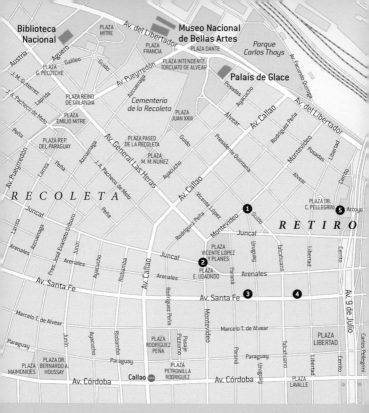

RETIRO

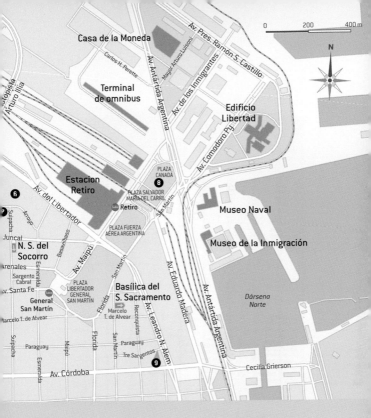

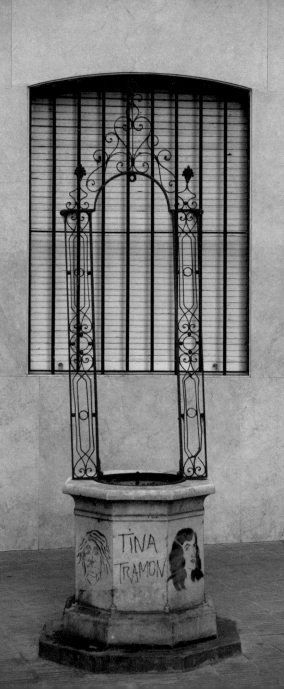

WATER TANK ON CALLE GUIDO

Calles Guido and Uruguay, Recoleta district
• Buses: 10, 37, 39, 60, 102, 106, 110, 129, 150, 152

> *The last water tank on a street*

On the corner of Calles Guido and Uruguay, in Recoleta district, a water tank standing on the pavement evokes memories of 18th-century Buenos Aires. These tanks were common in colonial times but very few exist today and the one in Recoleta is the only one that can still be seen *in situ*.

However, it is only a replica of the original which supplied a house in Recoleta, an area of farms and country retreats at the time. Over the years, the land was divided up and the district changed radically as generations of Porteños (inhabitants of Buenos Aires) came and went. In spite of the ban on water tanks in 1880, when mains water was connected, the one in Calle Guido was left standing.

In 2001, in an effort to highlight the cultural heritage of Buenos Aires, the city council had the original water tank moved to the patio of the Argentine Society of Writers in San Telmo, where it stands today. However, the locals in Recoleta were so upset that they demanded that it be put back: their wish was partially granted when a copy was placed there.

The water tank stands in front of a building that is covered, up to a height of 20 metres, in luxuriant vegetation, breaking the monotony of the cement. This may have been inspired by Le Corbusier's idea of a roof garden. The owner of the seventh floor of the building, Adrian Gonzalez, has designed a wooded landscape hanging on steel cables there.

THE CITY'S OTHER WATER TANKS

It is hard to find many examples of the old water tanks in Buenos Aires today as most of them gradually disappeared with the arrival of mains water. However, there are some in the Museo de Arte Hispanoamericano Isaac Fernández Blanco, in the Museo Argentino de Ciencias Naturales Bernardino Rivadavia and in the internal patio of the Casa Rosada. There is also one in the grounds of La Santa Casa de Ejercicios Espirituales (see p. 80), a Jesuit convent in Buenos Aires. The one in Patio Cabildo is still intact. Finally, in Recoleta district, apart from the one in Calle Guido, there are two others: one in the Cultural Centre and the other in the patio behind the Church of Nuestra Señora del Pilar.

A WORK BY MARTA MINUJÍN AT LE PONT CAFÉ ❷

Le Pont café
1300 Calle Montevideo (on the corner of Calle Juncal), Recoleta district
• Metro: line D, Callao station
• Buses: 10, 12, 39, 60, 106, 124, 152

> **One
> of the most unusual
> exchanges
> in the history of art**

There is a surprising story behind the mural painted by the avant-garde artist Marta Minujín on the walls of Le Pont café in the Recoleta area.

In 2011 Minujín, who used to drink about twenty coffees a day, offered to paint a mural in the café in exchange for free coffees for life. She sketched a scene with seven characters – four women and three men – painted in red, violet and black.

Minujín described her work as being a person standing alone in a multidirectional or paranoiac world: "We are all several people in one and we

change depending on the way that other people see us. [….] The look that we receive and the image that we give are not always the same."

The mural is part of a series of fragmented faces, an idea that came to Minujín in 1986 when she was working at Ezeiza Airport. "I was standing on some scaffolding when the boxer Carlos Monzon approached me to ask for my autograph. As we did not have any paper to hand, I painted on a plate. Since then I have done many others like that and I have even sold them," she said.

The Argentinian artist Marta Minujín was born in Buenos Aires in 1943. She is famous for her avant-garde works, produced mainly in the 1960s, '70s and '80s. She is a conceptual, pop and psychedelic artist and is seen as representing the dogma of the "baby-boomer" generation, which shook up the accepted social norms of society in the sixties by creating a counter-culture.

RUINS OF THE OLD TEATRO VERSAILLES

1445 Avenida Santa Fe
• Metro: line D, Callao station
• Buses: 10, 17, 39, 59, 101, 106, 150, 152

*A shop
in an old theatre*

According to a metal plaque at No. 1445 Avenida Santa Fe, the Kevington Teatro clothes shop was established here in December 2010. You would be wrong in thinking that this plaque was put up for advertising purposes. All previous tenants of this building, formerly the Teatro Versailles (Versailles Theatre), have also had to bow to this constraint. "So why was it put up?" you might ask.

After the 1995 coup d'état which overthrew Juan Domingo Perón, the Teatro Versailles (which had strong links with him) was forced to close down.

In the 1960s the place opened up again, but not as a theatre. It was renamed La Scala when a women's clothes shop took over a small part of the front of the old theatre. That is how most of the theatre and its features have remained intact to this very day: almost as if to pay silent homage to the stage where some of the great names of Argentina's play-acting world performed. Ángel Magaña gave the premiere of *Eyes Full of Love* here, and Tita Merello and the very young Lydia Lamaison were also applauded for their performances.

There is a certain amount of nostalgia surrounding the old theatre. At the Ateneo Gran Splendid bookshop further down the avenue, they will tell you how wonderful it once was. All the tenants who have occupied the building over the years seem to have respected the spirit of the place. We can still make out where the boxes were, and the clothes models standing there today remind us that audiences once gave the actors standing ovations.

Today, the daylight peeps through holes in the dome, which is decorated with acrylics. Off-stage, the old actors' lodges are being used for storage.

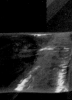

CASA DEL TEATRO

Teatro Regina
1243 Avenida Santa Fe
• Metro: line D, Tribunales station; line C, San Martin station
• Artists' Market for a month between July and August

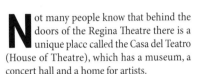

> *A refuge for retired artists*

Not many people know that behind the doors of the Regina Theatre there is a unique place called the Casa del Teatro (House of Theatre), which has a museum, a concert hall and a home for artists.

The ten-storey-high building was commissioned in the 1930s by the lyrical singer Regina Pacini (1871–1965), the wife of President Alvear. She wanted to create a place for retired artists similar to the retirement home set up by Giuseppe Verdi in Milan (the Casa Verdi) for penniless retired opera singers.

In 1938 the Casa del Teatro's first eight residents moved in. Over the last 70 years, the home has put up around 100 men and women from the world of theatre, some of whom had fallen out of the public eye at the end of a brilliant career. The film director Hugo Fregonese was one of these residents who, in spite of a successful career in Hollywood and Europe, ended up penniless in Argentina. Other residents included the television presenter Colomba Mario Amaya, a popular radio-theatre actor, and Carmen Lamas, one of the first stars and a member of the Maipu Theatre.

Although the centre itself is not open to the public, you may catch a glimpse of the residents (some more famous than others) while visiting the library or the museum.

The Casa del Teatro is funded by the city council in addition to contributions from the actors themselves, partners, company donations and fund-raising events and festivals.

The most famous event at the centre is the Feria de los Artistas (Artists' Market), where you can pick up all manner of cut-price articles (costumes, hats, gloves and jewellery) that once belonged to the artists. The market takes place every year and runs for a month between July and August. Any profits are used by the Casa del Teatro to improve the daily living conditions of its residents.

TROMPE-L'ŒIL OF THE HOUSE OF AUCHAS ❺

Calles Arroyo and Cerrito
• Buses: 62, 67, 92, 129, 130, 152

A false façade

On Plaza Cataluña, surrounded by Calles Arroyo and Cerrito, the back of a house is completely covered with an excellent *trompe-l'œil* of a lifelike wall with windows.

Barcelona's Plaza Catalunya is renowned as a popular meeting place, but its Buenos Aires equivalent is far from being a hit with tourists. It seems to have been swallowed up in the renovation work and forgotten.

This may well be why the Catalan painter Josep Niebla was commissioned to create an optical illusion here.

The mural stirred up some discussion among academics as to its aesthetic worth when it was unveiled at the beginning of the century. Some people thought that it should not be placed in the centre of the square and others even went as far as trying to ban it altogether.

In spite of its stormy debut, the *trompe-l'œil* is now included in many guided tours.

A REPLICA OF THE CANALETES FOUNTAIN

Plaza Cataluña also has a replica of the Font de Canaletes, one of the most famous fountains in the Catalan capital. It was presented to Buenos Aires in 1996 by the city of Barcelona.

GHOST OF THE FERNÁNDEZ BLANCO MUSEUM ❻

1422 Calle Suipacha
• Open Tues–Sun, 2–9pm
• Train: Mitre and Belgrano Norte lines, Retiro station

> *A ghost that has outshone the museum's collection*

The Museo de Arte Hispanoamericano Isaac Fernández Blanco (see box) is home to a legend that is so famous that, for the majority of visitors, it is more interesting than the collection itself. People are said to have witnessed sightings of a female dancer around the fountain in the museum's patio.

The first sightings date back as far as the 1940s, when Oliviero Girondo, who lived nearby, swore that he had had a very pleasant conversation with the young woman.

In the 1980s, sightings caused some puzzling discomfort to several members of the museum's staff and even to its director, who was in so much pain that he had to have an operation. Oddly enough, only the victim's sexual organs were affected: after some hesitation, the museum staff consulted a parapsychologist, who visited the place without knowing anything about this. He confirmed that the pain was caused by some paranormal force from beyond. He also mentioned a picture with a red-haired woman wearing a white toga.

In 1989 a ballet company was rehearsing in the patio when the ghost of the dancer appeared. Some of the dancers are said to have spoken to her. The urban legend goes that at the beginning of the 19th century, when the building was still a church, a 17-year-old woman died there from tuberculosis.

REMAINS OF THE FORMER ISRAELI EMBASSY ❼

Plaza Embajada de Israel
910 Calle Arroyo
• Metro: line C, San Martin station
• Buses: 17, 61, 92, 100, 140, 152

A stark, grey square with twenty-nine names engraved on a wall and a few trees representing life ... all this is a minute part of the memorial where the former Israeli embassy once stood forty years ago.

The symmetry of the lime trees reminds us that we are all equal in the face of death

Until 1992, the embassy stood at the intersection of Calle Suipacha and Calle Arroyo. In that year, at 2.30pm on 17 March, a blast from a suicide bomb destroyed the building, killing 29 people and injuring over 200.

The square was designed by the architects Gonzalo Navarro, Hugo A. Gutierrez, Patricio M. Navarro and Hector Farina. There are two large, intertwined plaques (one in Jerusalem stone and the other in Patagonian stone), surrounded by a small trench. The stone plaques symbolise the solidarity between Jewish and non-Jewish communities, united in the face of intolerance and incomprehension. In the centre, two rows of lime trees remind us that we are all equal in the face of death.

The names of all those killed in the bombing are written on a concrete slab on the lateral wall with a reminder of the terrorist attack (for which no one has ever been convicted). But the most striking evidence – kept intact since the explosion – can be found higher up: the damaged embassy's walls still bear the scars of a gaping wound that has never healed.

ISRAELI DIPLOMATIC MISSION IN BUENOS AIRES

In 1948 the embassy of Israel took up residence in a small, luxurious three-storey hotel situated in the heart of the diplomatic area close to the San Martin Palace, the seat of the Argentinian Chancellery.

The building had belonged to the wealthy Mihanovichs until a less-fortunate member of the family fell on hard times and was forced to sell it.

TOTEM POLE OF RETIRO

Plaza Canada
Avenidas Antártida Argentina and San Martin
• Metro: line C, Retiro station
• Train: Belgrano Norte, Mitre and San Martin, Retiro station

The totem pole can be found in the square opposite the Retiro bus terminus. It was erected in 1964 and was a gift to the city from the Canadian embassy in Buenos Aires, symbolising the friendship between the two countries. In return, the city named the square after its Canadian benefactors. Jorge Luis Borges is quoted as saying: "We know nothing of its cult; even more of a reason to dream about it at the waking of the day."

> **"We know nothing of its cult; even more of a reason to dream about it at the waking of the day"**

Over time, the 20-metre-high original fell into a state of disrepair and in 2008 it was taken down by the Ministry of Culture with a view to renovating it. After a considerable amount of research, the tribe that had made the totem pole was identified and another one was ordered. Stanley Hunt, the son of the man who had made the original pole, was commissioned to make a smaller model, standing 13 metres high. Erected in 2012, it is carved out of the painted trunk of a cedar tree and covered with images of the Kwakiutl people's mythological animals – the eagle, the sea lion, the otter, the whale, the beaver and a cannibal bird – in addition to Man, who is the creator of the rites, philosophy and founding legends of the Canadian aboriginal culture.

At the foot of the totem pole, there is a plaque with a extract from *Atlas* by Borges and Maria Kodama: "Our imagination would have us see a totem pole in exile, a totem pole which represents mythologies, tribes and even sacrifices."

SUNDIAL OF THE FORMER ITALO-ARGENTINE ❾
ELECTRIC COMPANY

352 Calle Tres Sargentos, Retiro district
• Buses: 6, 28, 56, 61, 93, 130, 132, 143, 152

Time told in the ancient way

This factory belonging to the former Italo-Argentine Electric Company dates from the beginning of the 20th century. The sundial at the top of the tower seems almost anachronistic in the age of touch screens and 5D technology.

Situated in Calle Tres Sargentos (a pedestrian passageway no more than two blocks in length), in the Retiro area, the old building is the work of Italian architect Juan Chiogna, who sought to adapt the European Gothic style for the industrial buildings of Buenos Aires.

The neo-medieval elegance of the façade allowed electricity to be installed in residential districts without disturbing the urban aesthetic or upsetting local residents.

The sundial is one of the city's few examples of this ancient measuring device. The handful of others are now in an extremely poor state of preservation.

The sundial in Plaza Lavalle, opposite the Palace of Justice, consists solely of a cement plinth, as the metal rod and part of the dial have been stolen. Another valuable example used to form part of the meteorological column in the Botanical Garden and showed the local time, as well as the time in eight other world cities, but it was vandalised so often that it was no longer considered worth repairing. Another, more modern example, made of marble and stainless steel, can be found opposite the planetarium.

The sundial situated on top of the old building, now owned by the electricity company Edesur, is still intact and worth a detour in its own right. What could be more pleasant than watching time go by?

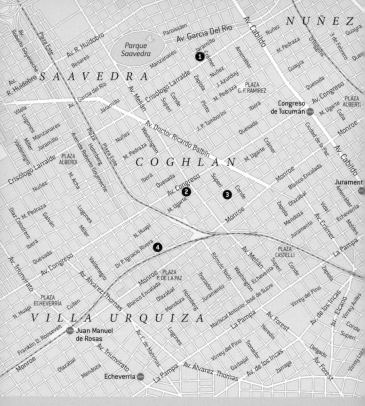

NORTH

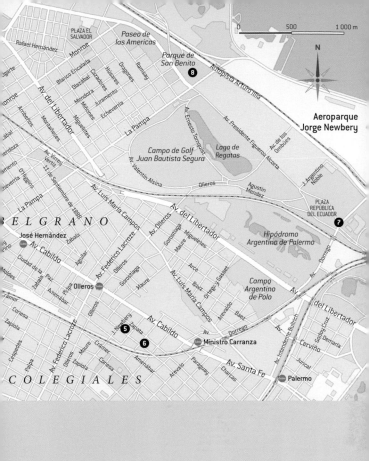

THE BLOCK OF HOUSES THAT LOOKS LIKE A COFFIN

❶

Avenidas Cabildo and Pico
• Buses: 19, 57, 60, 71, 130, 133, 152, 168, 184

> *There once was a bar named "The Coffin"*

O n Avenida Cabildo, just before Avenida General Paz, there is a narrow block of houses in the shape of a coffin. This urban curiosity is due to the line which was drawn at the junction of Avenidas San Isidro Labrador and Cabildo: it can be seen from a height or simply by studying a map. The space is so small that there is barely enough room for a shop. Today it is a shop that sells tyres, but in the 1920s it was a bar called "El Cajón" (The Coffin).

In order to explain its shape, some people like to tell tales of the bar's owner, said to be a ghost who had come back among the living: he had died (or rather, he had been declared dead) and while his coffin was being taken away for burial at Chacarita cemetery, it began to shake violently. A priest asked for the coffin to be opened and discovered that the "deceased" was still very much alive. He had, in fact, fallen into a state of catalepsy: a sudden and temporary loss of voluntary contractions of the limbs, which become stiff and motionless. The "deceased" is said to have been so grateful to the priest for saving his life that he had the building made in the shape of a coffin and opened a bar with the rather ominous name of "El Cajón".

This story was told by the famous Argentinian tango singer Edmundo Rivero in his book entitled *Una luz de almacén* (The Light of a Grocery). He describes a sort of inn which opened once or twice a week and was popular with workers from the nearby factories. El Cajón was famous for its affordable prices and its chicken casserole, which was served by the "ghost" and his family. In old photos of the place, we can make out the inn's terrace covered in advertisements. This was still very new in an area like Puente Saavedra, which was a shady and rather dangerous place at the time, better known for its card-sharpers and brothels.

VENTILATION FLUE OF COGHLAN

2900 Calle Washington and Avenida Congreso, Coghlan district
• Buses: 19, 41, 67, 76, 107, 169, 175
• Train: Mitre line, Coghlan station

A tower designed to ventilate the city's second largest sewer

F ar from the centre, at No. 2900 in Calle Washington, in the Coghlan area, a brick tower rises up, 35 metres high, like a "second obelisk".

It was built in 1914 as part of the old Sanitary Works of the Nation of Argentina.

Although it looks very much like a chimney, the tower was actually built to ventilate the city's second largest sewer, which ran under the Coghlan area. It is built in a typically British style, with its exposed brickwork.

This style is found throughout the area: on the San Patricio Church (Estomba y Echeverria), the schools, the public offices and the Pirovano Hospital.

This is why the city council declared the polygon formed by Calle Tronador, Calle Rivera (the first street to be paved in Buenos Aires in 1907) and Calle Washington to be an "Área de Protección Histórica" (Area of Historic Protection).

CENTRO ANA FRANK

3

2647 Calle Superí, Coghlan district
• Train: Mitre line, Coghlan station
• Buses: 19, 41, 67, 76, 107, 114, 133, 169, 175
• Visits: Tues–Sat 2pm–7pm. Bookings: + 54 11 3533-8505

> *A museum in a house used as a hiding place for opponents of the regime*

The Anne Frank Centre is situated in the Coghlan district and was opened at the beginning of 2009. It was set up as a replica of the house in Amsterdam where Anne Frank hid for two years and where she wrote her famous diary before being arrested by the Nazis.

Superí's house in Buenos Aires was also used as a hiding place: it is known locally as "Hilda's house" after the owner, who helped political dissidents to hide from the Triple A,* and then from the last dictatorship (1976–1983).

The first floor has an exhibition on the life of Anne Frank, with texts and photos. On the second floor, visitors can see an exact replica of the revolving bookcase used by the Frank family as a hiding place. Items of furniture from the kitchen, sitting room and Anne's bedroom are also on display here.

The aim of this reconstitution of the "Annex" (the nickname used by the Frank family) is to show the environment in which Anne Frank wrote her diary and to remember her so that we may reflect on the dangers of anti-Semitism, racism and discrimination and defend the values of freedom, equal rights and democracy.

> The house where the Frank family hid for two years from the Nazis in Amsterdam is visited each year by over a million people. It has become one of the most important international institutions for the promotion of programmes against discrimination and in support of human rights.

THE TALE OF THE PARROTS MURAL ❹

Calles Holmberg and Rivera, Villa Urquiza district
• Train: Mitre line, Coghlan and Luis M. Drago stations
• Buses: 19, 41, 71, 76, 114, 133

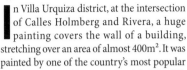

> *The city's largest mural*

I n Villa Urquiza district, at the intersection of Calles Holmberg and Rivera, a huge painting covers the wall of a building, stretching over an area of almost 400m². It was painted by one of the country's most popular graffiti artists and its surrealist title (*The Tale of the Parrots*) would no doubt have pleased André Breton.

The painting shows a giant skateboard with various things riding on it, such as a man's head with his tongue sticking out, a teenage figure with the body of a Greek god listening to a gramophone, and an enormous wasp alighting on a woman. On the right-hand side, we can see the smiling, albeit smaller, figure of the architect Clorindo Testa, who designed the National Library of the Republic of Argentina.

The mural, which is the largest in Buenos Aires, was painted by Martin Ron, an urban artist who has left his mark on the history of graffiti in the capital. He describes his artwork as "a vision between the unreal and the fantastic […] The head with its tongue hanging out, hair on end, and wide, staring eyes belongs to a friend of mine, Gabriel Dotta."

Ron worked on this mural from July to August 2013. The four-storey-high artwork is made up of two "canvases": one measures 14 metres high by 25 meters wide and the other 3.1 x 20. The mural means so much to the inhabitants of the building that they refused to let an advertisement be painted over part of it. The city took an active role in installing the mural and offered

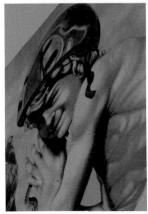

to create an arts centre in Villa Urquiza.

Thanks to a British journalist, Matt Fox-Tucker, who lives in Buenos Aires, a "graffiti hunt" tour is now on offer in the Saavedra, Palermo and Villa Urquiza districts. Fox-Tucker says that the Villa Urquiza area is particularly suitable as, when a project for the construction of a ring road fell through, it left behind a considerable amount of space on exposed walls that was ideal for this kind of artwork.

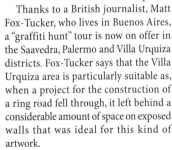

Martin Ron is also famous for his painting of the football player Carlos Tévez in the Fuerte Apache area of the city of Cuidadela.

HARE KRISHNA TEMPLE ❺

394/384 Cuidad de la Paz, Colegiales district
• Buses: 39, 41, 42, 57, 60, 68, 152, 161, 168, 194
• Daily ceremonies: 4.30am and 8.20am
• Altar of the temple open to the public until 12 noon

Mellow music, soft lighting, delicious food

In Belgrano, the front of the temple of the International Society for Krishna Consciousness (see box) is a vegetarian restaurant. Its followers never eat meat or eggs from any kind of animal.

The heart of the temple is the room at the back of the restaurant, where the ceremonies take place at set times: at 4.30am with Mangal Artik (morning ceremony) and at 8.20am with Guru Puja (a daily meeting in honour of the founder of the association).

The altar of the temple is open to the public until 12 noon, when it closes to make food offerings to the divinities. Among the various activities on offer are classes like Bhakti yoga, which uses time-honoured techniques to alleviate the stress of everyday life.

The restaurant attached to the temple is particularly pleasant: the mellow music, soft lighting and delicious food come together in a very harmonious way.

INTERNATIONAL SOCIETY FOR KRISHNA CONSCIOUSNESS

The International Society for Krishna Consciousness, widely known by its acronym ISKCON (the members are commonly called "Hare Krishna" due to the mantras they chant), is a current of Hinduism which is part of the Bhakti movement, dedicated to Lord Krishna, considered as God, the Supreme Lord.

The movement was founded in 1966 in New York by A.C. Bhaktivedanta Swami Prabhupada (1896–1977), a Hindu spiritual master from east Bengal. There are more than 150 Krishna temples run by ISKCON throughout the world; there are believed to be around 3,000 Hare Krishnas in Argentina.

THE CITY'S "FIXED POINTS"

Calles Zapata and Ciudad de La Paz
• Metro: line D, Carranza station

A t the crossroads of Calles Zapata and Ciudad de La Paz, keep an eye out for a small metal plaque on the wall with the following rather enigmatic inscription: "Municipality, Land registry, Levelling". The three words are written under one another. This is what is called a "fixed point". In the past

Remnants of an urban planning scheme

there were many such markers throughout Buenos Aires and there are still some in the areas outside the centre, but they are fast disappearing as the city grows and new buildings are erected.

These "fixed points" can generally be found 1 metre up from the ground: they are bronze rectangular markers made to last and resist vandalism. They are very much part of the city's "archaeological signature", as are the concrete blocks with horizontal slits that were used as letter boxes.

"Fixed points", otherwise known as land registry levelling, were markers placed by the Military Geographical Institute to indicate the height of the land in relation to Sea-level Zero. They date back to the 1920s in Buenos Aires and are part of several methods used by the MGI to take measurements.

They were an essential way of understanding the country's geography and collecting altimetric data, which was used to find the city's highest point and give an accurate picture of its topography.

SUIZA Y ARGENTINA UNIDAS SOBRE EL MUNDO SCULPTURE

❼

3700 Avenida Dorrego, Palermo district
• Buses: 34, 37, 57, 130, 152, 160

"
The most erotic sculpture in Buenos Aires

The "Switzerland and Argentina United Worldwide" sculpture may seem very daring for a monument from the beginning of the 20th century: two naked women holding hands and kissing each other on the mouth. But don't be deceived: it is not what it seems at first sight. Far from being a plea for sexual liberation or lesbianism, the statue is simply meant to symbolise the fraternity between the two countries.

It was sculpted by Paul Amlhen and was presented to Argentina by the Swiss Philanthropic Society for the 1810 centenary celebrations. The same artist also created a monument to celebrate shooting, the national sport of Switzerland. When the statue was inaugurated on 7 June 1914, it caused a stir, even if no one dared question this rather odd tribute to the Swiss.

The work, which stands over 10 metres tall, is made of bronze and granite and weighs an imposing 50 tonnes. It was brought to Buenos Aires on a steamship from Europe, in several pieces and packed in 70 boxes. Once assembled, the statue caused great admiration but also some shocked reactions as it was finally revealed: two magnificent women sitting on a sphere holding hands and kissing each other on the mouth with a sort of Cupid on horseback riding above them, as an allegory of the fraternity binding these two peoples.

The statue's suggestive nature was said to have caused some flushed cheeks among female passers-by in its time. What looks like a Cupid is, in reality, no more than a metaphor for shooting; and the sphere upon which the women are sitting depicts them emerging from the world globe to illustrate the union between the two countries.

Seen in this light, the allegory does not seem so shocking, even if the kiss still upsets some of today's visitors.

FLOATING STATUE IN PARQUE DE LA MEMORIA

8

6745 Calle Costanera Norte Rafael Obligado
• Open daily 10am–6pm
• Train: Belgrano Norte line, Scalabrini Ortiz station
• Buses: 28, 33, 37, 42, 107, 160

> *Silhouette of a teenager who went missing at the age of 14*

At the end of Paseo Parque de la Memoria, there is a statue of a teenager floating on the Rio de la Plata. It symbolises the scars left by the last military dictatorship's spine-chilling relationship with the river into which the bodies of hundreds of victims were thrown.

The statue represents the body of a boy who was only 14 when he was executed. Claudia Fontes' work is entitled *Reconstrucción del Retrato de Pablo Míguez* (Reconstruction of the Portrait of Pablo Míguez) and was specially designed to float on the Rio de la Plata, in order, as the artist puts it, to convey the concepts of appearing and disappearing.

There is another statue in the park in memory of the victims of State terror between 1969 and 1983. It is composed of four concrete commemorative slabs measuring 420 metres long, with 30,000 plaques (made of Patagonian porphyry) hanging on them. Only 9,000 of them are engraved with the names of those who went missing or who were assassinated. They are classified by year of death and in alphabetical order and also give the age of the victims and whether they were pregnant.

The list of names was started in 1998, using several sources such as human rights organisations' reports and data collected by the Mothers of the Plaza de Mayo. New investigations have been carried out recently and there have been several trials for crimes against humanity – these have helped to uncover more disappearances and assassinations. If these recent events are anything to go by, it seems that there are many more names to be added and the monument is sadly far from finished.

THE WORK ENTITLED "*30,000*"

"*30,000*" is the name of a work by Nicolas Guagnini (b. 1966). It is composed of twenty-five painted steel columns which make up a human face representing the artist's father who went missing in 1977.
The columns form a prism and the face is revealed only to those who look at it from a particular angle.

PALERMO AND RECOLETA

SCULPTURE OF LITTLE RED RIDING HOOD

Plaza Sicilia, Palermo Woods
Avenue Sarmiento, between Figueroa Alcorta and Libertador avenues
• Bus 10, 37, 57, 67, 102, 130, 160

*Lost
in the woods...*

The mythical character from the world of children's literature, Little Red Riding Hood, has her own magical statue in Buenos Aires. Sculpted in white marble by the French national Jean Carlus, it was acquired by the city of Buenos Aires in 1937.

Originally installed on Plaza Lavalle in the Tribunales area, it was moved during the 1970s to its current location in Parque Tres de Febrero.

The famous little girl with the curly hair is depicted in the middle of a thick copse, dressed in her hood and cape, carrying her wicker basket. The ferocious wolf skulks by her side, and the scene surprises those unexpectedly confronted by it.

Hidden at the edge of Plaza Sicilia, the statue unfortunately represents an easy target for vandals. Several years ago, it had to be urgently "admitted" to a statue restoration centre. It was damaged beyond recognition on arrival and the wolf had lost an ear. It was saved by work carried out by the restorers and it can now be admired every day at leisure by anyone taking a walk in the Palermo Woods.

In Buenos Aires there is also a Caperucita ("little hood") alley, in the Chacabuco area. A single city block in length, it is found between Picheuta and Avenida Del Barco Centenera, on a level with number 1650 of either street, and was given this name by ordinance no. 1424 of 30 December 1925.

THE ONLY MONUMENT IN THE WORLD DEDICATED TO LITTLE RED HOOD?

A certain local chauvinism has led some to claim that this is the only monument in the world dedicated to Little Red Riding Hood. In reality, there are other versions on public view in Australia, Germany, Russia and Spain.

"SCENT OF FORGIVENESS" TREE

Plaza Sicilia, Bosques de Palermo
Avenidas del Libertador and Sarmiento
• Buses: 37, 57, 67, 130

> *It was under this tree that Rosas' daughter begged her father to spare her friend Camila O'Gorman*

A frail little tree has been standing in the Palermo Woods on the Plaza Sicilia since the beginning of the 19th century. Known as "the scent of forgiveness" tree, it is said to have been planted by Manuelita, the daughter of Juan Manuel de Rosas (governor of the Province of Buenos Aires, 1829–1832 and 1835–1852).

Manuelita was great friends with Camila O'Gorman, a well-brought up young lady who fell deeply in love with a priest with whom she later eloped. Camila sent a message to her friend, asking her to convince her father to use his influence to let them leave. But when Manuelita told him, Juan Manuel de Rosas flew into a rage and demanded that the elopers be executed – despite the fact that Camila was eight months pregnant at the time.

The story goes that Manuelita begged her friend's father to spare his daughter under this tree (known also as "Manuelita's scent"), in the shade of which the two friends had often chatted and drunk *mate*.

Today the tree is surrounded by a fence (erected in 1974), with a commemorative plaque to keep the legend alive.

THE PALERMO DISTRICT

Palermo was a large area made up of secondary homes and farms until 1838, when Juan Manuel de Rosas started acquiring the land.

From 1839 to 1852, the governor lived in a colonial-style property that he had built with watchtowers on every corner. His country home stood on what is now the crossroads between Avenidas del Libertador and Sarmiento.

Today, one of the entrances to the imposing *estancia* (ranch) leads to the town zoo. The property was finally demolished in 1899 but, according to architectural historians, its remains can still be seen in the park.

BELL OF PEACE ③

Japanese Garden
2966 Avenida Casares
• Open daily 10am–6pm
• Metro: line D, Scalabrini Ortiz station
• Buses: 37, 57, 67, 102, 130

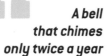

A bell that chimes only twice a year

The "bell of peace" can be found in the Japanese Garden on Avenida Casares, just a few hundred metres from the emblematic red bridge called Taiko-Bashi, which leads to the traditional "Isle of Gods". It is protected by a 5-metre-high wooden structure and no one can touch it without some kind of authorisation.

There are only sixteen bells of its kind in the world. The one in Japan is called Tsuri-Gane, but unlike the bell in Buenos Aires, it does not have a clapper and a wooden stick is used to make it ring.

The Buenos Aires "bell of peace" is decorated with medals and coins from over 100 different countries. It was inaugurated in February 1998 to

commemorate the anniversary of the signing of the treaty of friendship between Argentina and Japan.

The bell only chimes twice a year: once on 21 September, when all the other bells of peace across the world ring to celebrate International Peace Day; and again to celebrate the end of the year and the beginning of the new one. The latter comes from an old Buddhist tradition which says that Man can recognise and then free himself of his 108 sins by ringing the bell 108 times.

NEARBY

Near the bell tower, if you follow the path leading away from the lake, you will see the gingko biloba, also known as the "silver apricot tree". This tree has existed since the Jurassic period and it managed to survive and grow back after the atomic bombs were dropped on Japan during the Second World War. The Japanese worship it for the very reason that it is a wonderful symbol of rebirth after disaster. On a windy day, the leaves are shaken from it in a kind of silvery shower.

DE LA PAZ MUNDIAL

MONUMENT TO A POLICE DOG ④

Mounted Police barracks
3700 Avenida Figueroa Alcorta
• Buses: 37, 67, 102, 130

> *Chonino, the most decorated dog in the Canine Division of the National Police Force*

A bronze statue in the grounds of the National Police Force headquarters pays tribute to Chonino, a heroic dog who died on the job. It shows the animal standing on a pedestal on Avenida Casares, just before Avenida Figueroa Alcorta, and gives the impression that the most decorated Alsatian in the Canine Division is still on guard.

Chonino was only a puppy when he was recruited by the Armed Forces and began his training as a guard dog. He had "worked" for six years until one fateful afternoon on 2 June 1983, when he was selected for a patrol with two non-commissioned officers. During their round, one of the policemen was injured in a shooting incident. Chonino jumped on the villain and tore off a piece of his jacket before being shot by him in the chest. The police later managed to arrest the culprit, using the identity papers that they found wedged in the dog's jaw.

Chonino's body has been conserved at the National Police Force. The statue was erected, in his memory, at the headquarters of the division in which he served.

A DOG WHICH GAVE ITS NAME TO A STREET AND INSPIRED "NATIONAL DOG DAY"

Tucked away at the back of the Mounted Police barracks, between its surrounding walls and the tracks of the San Martin railway line, there is a small cobbled lane with no pavements called "Pasaje Chonino". In 1989 the city council changed its name as a tribute to the bravest dog in Buenos Aires. It also created "National Dog Day", which is celebrated every year on 2 June.

CONFUSING SYMBOLISM OF THE ROOSEVELT ❺ MONUMENT

Avenidas Colombia and Cervino, Palermo district
• Buses: 10, 37, 57, 67, 130

In 1949, at the request of the United States embassy, a monument to President Franklin D. Roosevelt was erected in Plaza Seeber, on Avenida Colombia, just opposite the embassy.

This monument, however, is rather ambiguous. It is difficult to understand what the popular Argentinian sculptor, José Fioravanti – already famous for creating the National Flag monument – had in mind when he designed it.

> *The President of the United States sitting between fascism and liberty*

The sculpture stands on a marble base with three pedestals, each holding a human figure made of bronze. The highest, central pedestal shows Roosevelt sitting on a throne. Achieving a life-like sculpture of such a great democrat, and four times US president, was a real challenge for Fioravanti.

Although the central figure might seem a logical way to portray Roosevelt himself, the figures representing a naked man and a naked woman on the other two pedestals are rather baffling. The male statue is called *Combate contra el mal* (Fight against Evil) and shows an Adonis holding a decapitated snake. A strangely prophetic metaphor, according to the public heritage expert Juan Antonio Lazara, who was quoted as saying: "In contrast to the tradition in the history of sculpture, which generally represents the allegory of destiny in the form of a viper who defends the righteous, in this instance, [the snake] is defeated." Lazara therefore interprets this symbol as an allegory of the defeat of fascism in the Second World War by the Allied forces led by Roosevelt.

The figure of the woman called *Libertad de religión* (Freedom of Religion), on the other side, forms a striking contrast: it is almost erotic, with the woman holding on to a dove that is about to fly away. All these details seem to suggest that it represents peace. The monument therefore seems to be evoking two apparently antagonistic symbols which could, in some ways, be seen as complementary: "democracy–liberty–peace" on one hand and on the other "fascism–fate–war".

COMMEMORATIVE PLAQUE OF ALEJANDRO FERREIRO

6

2846 Avenida Scalabrini Ortiz, Palermo district
• Metro: line D, Scalabrini Ortiz station

Palermo's most popular down-and-out

If you go to the intersection between Avenidas Scalabrini Ortiz and Santa Fe, you can't miss the commemorative plaque that reads: "Here lived Alejandro Ferreiro, dearly loved by us all, for twelve years."

This modest commemorative monument was erected in October 2013 by the local residents in memory of a down-and-out who had died there on 7 September.

Alejandro Ferreiro, aka Pechito, was a particularly well-liked local figure in the Palermo district. He never begged for money and he ran errands for people in exchange for a few spare coins. He lived among his dogs, a mattress, a small television set, a carafe and a stereo that he used to hold karaokes at weekends.

Pechito had two "homes": the doorstep of a bank and the roof of a shop. When it rained he took refuge in the shop entrance and at other times he lived in the doorway of the bank. "I'd rather people called me poor or a vagabond than a tramp. People like me because I'm respectful and charismatic," he said during one of the very few interviews he gave.

One day Pechito disappeared into thin air. His closest friends checked all the hospitals and police stations in the area and finally found him in the Rivadavia hospital where he had been placed by social workers, two days previously, under mysterious circumstances. He had been taken there in a very worrying state and finally died there from respiratory problems some time later. He was 39.

A STATUE OF THE MOST POPULAR DOWN-AND-OUT IN ARGENTINA'S COMIC STRIPS

A sculpture of a vagabond and his dog, Diogenes – the main characters in the famous comic strip, *Diógenes y El Linyera* – has been erected under a tree in the Parque de las Mujeres Argentinas (Park of the Women of Argentina) in Puerto Madero. This work by Pablo Irrgang pays homage to the Uruguayan illustrator, Tabaré Gómez Laborde, who created *Diógenes y El Linyera*, which was published on a daily basis for almost forty years on the back page of the *Clarín* newspaper. It is now included in the "comic-strip sculptures tour" of Buenos Aires.

QUINQUELA IN THE METRO

• Metro: line D, Plaza Italia station

I f you go onto the main platform of the Plaza Italia metro station, one of the busiest in Buenos Aires, you can actually walk over a work of art by Benito Quinquela Martin, the popular Argentinian painter (see box).

Walk over a famous Argentinian painter's work

Adapted from a sketch dating back to 1939 called *La Descarga de los convoyes* (Downloading the Convoys), the work measures 6.35 x 4.23 metres. It was made in polychrome cement by Constantino Yuste and depicts everyday scenes with Riachuelo workers, a typical theme of Quinquela Martin, who was brought up in the La Boca area.

> The Riachuelo river stretches for some 64 km; its source lies on the outskirts of Buenos Aires and it flows into the Rio de la Plata. It forms the southern border of the autonomous city of Buenos Aires.

BENITO QUINQUELA MARTIN

The Argentinian artist Benito Quinquela Martin (1890–1977), aka "The Coal Merchant", is famous for his paintings of everyday life in the docklands. He was an orphan who used the name of his adopted parents and found the inspiration to create his work from his difficult upbringing.

Totally self-taught and with no technical knowledge of drawing, he was an intuitive painter, inspired by a world of docks and fishing boats. He was obsessed by his work and very productive.

He has left some 500 works, thousands of sketches and drawings on canvas, cardboard and wood as well as wall paintings.

COLUMN FROM ROME'S IMPERIAL FORUM

4000 Avenida Santa Fe
Plaza Italia
• Metro: line D, Plaza Italia station
• Buses: 10, 12, 15, 29, 39, 41, 55

Not many people know that there is an authentic relic of Ancient Rome hidden away on one of the busiest avenues in Buenos Aires. The column, which is 2,000 years old, was taken from an emblematic Roman forum and given to the city by the Italian government in 1955.

The city's oldest monument

What better place for this piece of architectural history – and the city's oldest monument – than Plaza Italia? But beware: you will need to keep your wits about you to find it in the midst of thirty bus lines and the hustle and bustle of heavy traffic, crowds of pedestrians and noisy car horns. Finding this marble column (1.90 metres high and 55 metres in diameter) beside the rotunda, where Avenida Sarmiento comes to an end at Calle Thames, can feel like a treasure hunt.

As this particular treasure stood in the open air, it suffered considerable damage. The damage was so severe that, after the bronze plaque was stolen, all that remained to be seen was a neglected stone post covered in soot.

The Roman and Latium Association of Argentina – an institution representing expatriates from Rome – warned the city council that the monument was in need of renovation. It was restored to its former glory in time for the celebration of the 150th anniversary of the unification of Italy.

SATURNALIA

9

Botanical Garden, 3951 Avenida Santa Fe
- Open Mon–Fri 8am–7pm, Sat–Sun 9.30am–7pm. Admission free
- Metro: line D, Plaza Italia station
- Buses: 15, 39, 59, 64, 93, 118, 152

> *The statue that was banned for half a century*

One of the numerous statues in the Botanical Garden represents a group of drunk people: some are enjoying themselves while others seem about to drop to their knees. This sculpture by the Italian Ernesto Biondi is a copy of the original, which was created in 1909 to celebrate the first centenary of May 1810 Week – this paved the way for the Argentinian War of Independence.

Regrettably, the sculpture was confiscated by Customs and kept out of sight until 1912 as the authorities considered it provocative. *Saturnalia* represents the Ancient Roman Bacchanalia: festivities where slaves and masters rubbed shoulders while taking part in a frenetic celebration of the God Bacchus. These festivities would last several days during which even the most unruly behaviour was tolerated.

When permission was finally given to release the statue, it was on the express condition that it would not be put on public display. The diplomat Hernan Cullen Ayerza, who had recuperated the statue, had no other choice but to display it in the grounds of his very own house.

When Ayerza died in 1957, the sculpture was donated to the National Museum of Fine Arts in accordance with his last wishes. But even then, the museum found it impossible to forget the statue's scandalous past and it was hidden away in one of the city's depots. It was only in 1963, when Arturo Illia became president, that Argentinians were able to admire the sculpture for the very first time. Fifty years after its arrival in the country, it was displayed at the Cuidad Club in Buenos Aires and then at the San Martin Cultural Centre.

It was, however, censured yet again after Videla's coup d'état in 1976 and sent back to the city's archives. Here it was left to gather dust until it was eventually brought back out into the light of day in the 1980s. The fully restored statue now stands in the Botanical Garden, where visitors can see two priests enjoying the festivities alongside a young patriot, a prostitute, a gentlemen, a wrestler, a slave, a soldier and a musician.

ROBERTO ARLT PASSAGEWAY

1959 Gurruchaga, Palermo district
• Metro: line D, Plaza Italia station

> *A secret*
> *passageway*

I n the very heart of the Palermo district, at No. 1959 Gurruchaga, what looks like a garage – fenceless and partially overgrown with trees – opens out into a secret passageway among a huddle of houses. It is barely noticeable as it leads nowhere and is not shown on the town maps.

This passageway, which dates back to the beginning of the last century, is no more than 3 metres wide and comes from a time when third-party rights of way still existed in Buenos Aires. The story goes that in 1910, Shine, an English engineer working for the British Railway Company, bought the whole plot in order to divide it up and build three luxury houses on it (they were to be the area's most imposing dwellings) with a view to renting them to well-to-do families. A lane was planned to give access to three other houses, designed for Shine and his family.

A short time later, Elizabeth Shine, the entrepreneur's granddaughter, moved into one of these more humble houses with her husband Roberto Arlt, after secretly marrying him. Arlt was an attractive, smooth-talking 40-year-old, author of *El Juguete rabioso* (The Mad Toy) and the star journalist of the newspaper *El Mundo*. His considerable writing talents could not, however, hide his pitiful track record as an unfaithful husband. This is why the passageway was named after him.

Of all the Buenos Aires *Aguafuertes* (see box), there is no better example than this little spot where time seems to stand still, full of magic and shrouded in mystery. Not so long ago, locals walking past it took a wide berth of the house on the passageway. They say that a strange man went mad after living there on his own with his dogs. No one seems to know who lives there now.

Roberto Arlt's *Aguafuertes porteñas* (Etchings from Buenos Aires) are short stories of everyday life in the city, giving brief insights into the Argentinian capital, its inhabitants, its customs and its way of life.

JULIO SOSA   "El Varón del Tango"

POR LA IDENTIDAD CIUDADANA
POR EL TANGO RIOPLATENSE
¡MUCHAS GRACIAS "VARON"!

2007

Tangueros y Tanguistas

1949   1964

58 AÑOS DE TU
LLEGADA A LA
ARGENTINA

43 AÑOS DE TU
DESAPARICION
FISICA

DONACION
PABLO BUFFA
RICARDO ALBANESE
19-10-2007

SATURNALIA

Botanical Garden, 3951 Avenida Santa Fe
• Open Mon–Fri 8am–7pm, Sat–Sun 9.30am–7pm. Admission free
• Metro: line D, Plaza Italia station
• Buses: 15, 39, 59, 64, 93, 118, 152

> **The statue that was banned for half a century**

One of the numerous statues in the Botanical Garden represents a group of drunk people: some are enjoying themselves while others seem about to drop to their knees. This sculpture by the Italian Ernesto Biondi is a copy of the original, which was created in 1909 to celebrate the first centenary of May 1810 Week – this paved the way for the Argentinian War of Independence.

Regrettably, the sculpture was confiscated by Customs and kept out of sight until 1912 as the authorities considered it provocative. *Saturnalia* represents the Ancient Roman Bacchanalia: festivities where slaves and masters rubbed shoulders while taking part in a frenetic celebration of the God Bacchus. These festivities would last several days during which even the most unruly behaviour was tolerated.

When permission was finally given to release the statue, it was on the express condition that it would not be put on public display. The diplomat Hernan Cullen Ayerza, who had recuperated the statue, had no other choice but to display it in the grounds of his very own house.

When Ayerza died in 1957, the sculpture was donated to the National Museum of Fine Arts in accordance with his last wishes. But even then, the museum found it impossible to forget the statue's scandalous past and it was hidden away in one of the city's depots. It was only in 1963, when Arturo Illia became president, that Argentinians were able to admire the sculpture for the very first time. Fifty years after its arrival in the country, it was displayed at the Cuidad Club in Buenos Aires and then at the San Martin Cultural Centre.

It was, however, censured yet again after Videla's coup d'état in 1976 and sent back to the city's archives. Here it was left to gather dust until it was eventually brought back out into the light of day in the 1980s. The fully restored statue now stands in the Botanical Garden, where visitors can see two priests enjoying the festivities alongside a young patriot, a prostitute, a gentlemen, a wrestler, a slave, a soldier and a musician.

HOMAGE TO JULIO SOSA

Intersection of Avenidas Figueroa Alcorta and Mariscal Ramon Castilla,
Palermo Chico district
• Buses: 10, 37, 60, 92, 102, 110, 130
• Train: Belgrano Norte line, Salidas station

> *A homage to the "tango male"*

At the intersection of Avenidas Figueroa Alcorta and Mariscal Ramon Castilla, keep your eyes peeled for an unassuming ceramic plaque, laid in memory of a dramatic event that occurred on 25 November 1964.

This is where Julio Sosa, aka "El Varón del Tango" (the tango male), Argentina's mythical tango singer, crashed into a block of concrete which had been placed there to protect the traffic lights. He died some 24 hours later.

Sosa had just been singing the *La Gayola* tango at Radio Splendid. With hindsight, the lyrics of the song seem strangely ominous: *"Pa'que no me falten flores cuando esté dentro el cajón"* (So that there are enough flowers when I'm lying in a wooden box). On his way out of the recording studio, Sosa had stopped off for a few drinks at a friend's stag party. He had three people in his car: Raul Secorun, his agent's son, a Chilean named Contreras, and the singer Marta Quintana. The two men got out of the car shortly afterwards – they probably thought that Sosa had had too much to drink and was driving recklessly. Quintana stayed in the car and she and Sosa had a nightcap in a bar near her house. "El Varón del Tango" then got back in his car and drove down Avenida Figueroa Alcorta.

Forty years after Sosa's death, one of the singer's fans, Ricardo Albanese, had this ceramic plaque laid in homage to him where the accident took place. He has also created a small private museum dedicated to the singer in his house in the Barracas area. It has clothes, records and original magazines and

newspapers as well as some of the late singer's personal effects, mostly donated by his widow. One of the most moving souvenirs is the steering wheel of the Fissoré DKW coupé in which Sosa was to meet his death. Although the museum is not yet open to the public, Albanese is currently working on this project with the city council.

HALTE WITOLD GOMBROWICZ

2525 Avenida Las Heras
• Buses: 10, 37, 60, 92, 110, 118, 130
• Open Mon–Fri 9am–9pm, Sat and Sun 12am–9pm

A
make-shift library

On Avenida Las Heras, a short walk from the National Library, there is a small building sitting opposite Plaza del Lector. It is called the Apeadero Gombrowicz ("Halte Gombrowicz"), a strange name which is little used these days.

In the beginning, this place, which forms an arcade, was home to a joint project between the National Library and the publishing company El Zorzal. Called the Máquina del Bicentenario, it was a jukebox-like dispenser for books that were no bigger than a pack of cigarettes. In this way, about 2,000 copies of each book were distributed.

The project started by publishing the works of ten authors, among whom were Lucio V. Mansilla, Walt Whitman and Domingo Faustino Sarmiento. In 2007 the "machine", which was in fact a recycled vending machine, delivered one book for every peso spent. The intention was to increase the number of authors in the list, but the contraption very quickly found itself gathering dust and it was soon relegated to the basement of the National Library.

Today the building (measuring 5 x 5 metres) has been converted into a make-shift library where passers-by can stop off for a quick read. It is the only one of its kind in Buenos Aires. Its white walls are covered in shelves laden with books published exclusively by the National Library. Readers can either sit comfortably on a sofa in cosy surroundings for a while or borrow a book as they would do in a more traditional library.

The make-shift library was named after Witold Gombrowicz (1904–1969) as a tribute to the Polish author, who spent twenty-five years of his life in Argentina.

POPEMOBILE OF THE AUTOMOBILE CLUB OF ARGENTINA

1850 Avenida del Libertador
• Open Mon–Fri 10am–5.30pm. Free admission

> *A 1981 Ford crane truck*

On the first floor of the Automobile Club of Argentina (ACA), there is a vehicle used by Pope John Paul ll when he first visited Argentina in 1982 (during the Falklands/Malvinas War).

When John Paul ll announced that he was going to Buenos Aires, the city's archbishop ordered a vehicle from the ACA that would enable the crowds to see the pope during his visit. The Popemobile (with the number plate SCV 1, which stands for *Status Civitatis Vaticanae*, Vatican City State) was designed from a 1981 Ford crane truck to which various modifications were made in compliance with the security constraints imposed by the Vatican.

A special team was appointed by the ACA to make the modifications. Considering the importance of the vehicle and the very tight schedule for its completion, they worked non-stop and free of charge in order to finish it on time. The workers were joined by a company specialising in metalwork and a glass panel maker who supplied the necessary material to build the Popemobile at no extra cost.

As well as the Popemobile, the museum has a collection of vintage cars, racing cars, old photos, advertisements, road signs, trophies, helmets, some of Juan Manuel Fangio's personal belongings and the very first driving licence given to a woman in 1912.

During his stay in Buenos Aires, after saying mass in Lujan, Jean Paul ll rode back into town in a Mercedes Benz 1114/48 bus on the 501 line, accompanied by a group of journalists. Some souvenirs of this particular event are also on display in the museum.

During the pope's second visit in April 1987, the Popemobile was made from a Renault Trafic, which is now on display in the Museum of Industry in Cordoba.

STATUE OF RAOUL GUSTAF WALLENBERG

Avenidas Figueroa Alcorta and Austria, Recoleta district
• Buses: 17, 61, 62, 67, 92, 93, 124, 130

> *A hero without a grave who saved thousands of Hungarian Jews from the Holocaust*

On the edge of Plaza República Oriental del Uruguay, at the intersection of Avenidas Figueroa Alcoa and Austria, stands a very discreet statue of Raoul Gustaf Wallenberg (1912–1945) that was erected in 1998. It can easily be missed as there is no pedestal for this statue of a man holding his coat and looking down. The only reference to Wallenberg is engraved on the wall behind.

Wallenberg was the rich Swedish heir to his family's industrial and financial empire. He spent much of his career doing business in various different countries before being sent to Budapest during the Second World War. There he became a diplomat and was given a mission to save Hungarian Jews.

Survivors have born witness to this period, telling how Wallenberg issued them with false temporary passports, claiming to the authorities that they were Swedish citizens waiting to be sent back to their country. He operated just like Oskar Schindler (1908–1974), the German industrialist who saved the lives of 1,100 Polish Jews. It is said that Wallenberg even managed to save people by boarding the trains taking them to the extermination camps.

The last heard of Wallenberg was when he was arrested by the KGB in 1945 and accused of spying for the United States. No one really knows how he died and this is why he is sometimes referred to as "the man without a grave".

The sculpture in Recoleta is a replica of the work of a Scottish artist, Philip Jackson, which stands in Great Cumberland Place in London, the city that became home to many of the people Wallenberg saved.

There is no general agreement about just how many people Raoul Wallenberg saved. The figure ranges from 30,000 to 100,000 people saved in Budapest. Whatever the actual figure may be, Wallenberg is, without a doubt, one of the unsung heroes of the Second World War.

FUENTE DE POESÍA ⑮

2500 Calle Agüero
• Buses: 10, 37, 41, 60, 92, 108, 110, 124

> **Poetry creates its own antibodies**

Today, all that is left of the *Fountain of Poetry* on Calle Agüero, between Avenidas Las Heras and del Libertador, is a fountain full of stagnant water and a plaque engraved with the names of the two artists who created it: Sylvia Perl and Enrique Banfi. Every night, from 1997 to 2001, eighty poems were projected onto the neighbouring wall; then, in turn, they were reflected in the water, making it seem as if the words were swimming in and out of the ripples.

Verses by Borges, Raul Gonzalez Tunon, Pablo Neruda, Oliviero Girondo, Juan Gelman, Enrique Molina and many more were thus projected by a system which came on automatically at nightfall.

The verses changed every minute "so that the city could be used as a creative stage", as their creators put it. Thanks to this work, the artists became famous throughout the world of Art.

Although it had initially been meant as a temporary work of art, the show went on for four years and when Sylvia Perl was asked why she thought this "poetry machine" had lasted so long, she gave this rather enigmatic reply: "Poetry creates its own antibodies."

The show was forced to stop suddenly at the end of 2001 when the projector was stolen, probably by New Year's Eve revellers. There was some talk of replacing it, but the project fell through as the artists had left Argentina.

The writer Edgard Shaw wrote about the work: "Poetry which is trapped inside a book, crushed by an infinite number of similar works, loses its freshness, its taste and becomes lifeless. When a poem is free to leave, and stay out to all hours, to weave an emotional spell on lovers and loners alike, its message is passed on from person to person. Enrique Banfi and Sylvia Perl have succeeded in unchaining poetry from its shackles and from its rigid frame […] These are the gestures which relieve us of the town's hostility."

THE STREET IN THE FORM OF A STAIRCASE

2300 Calle Arjonilla, Recoleta district
• Metro: line D, Agüero station
• Buses: 10, 37, 41, 60, 108, 110, 124

A taste of Paris in the heart of Recoleta

Don't miss the discreet little plaque on Calle Arjonilla indicating this unusual street, which runs from the foot of the Bartolomé Mitre monument and ends just opposite the National Library in Calle Agüero. The street is, in reality, a staircase, 50 metres wide, composed of 33 steps, 2 landings and a miniature boulevard, which stands out from the more typical streets to be found in Buenos Aires.

The area that it runs through is known as "La Isla" (The Island) and it is only accessible on foot: the paths leading up to it come together in a rotunda and the place rises up among trees, old-fashioned street lamps and balustrades.

La Isla is one of the most elegant and desirable areas in Buenos Aires.

When the city council launched the idea of a "district park" with a view over the river in 1906, it contacted a French specialist named Joseph-Antoine Bouvard, the administrative director of the Department of Architecture of Paris.

He was commissioned to trace the lines of the streets, the terraces and the three staircases, in addition to drawing up plans for the current Plaza Mitre.

Also in La Isla, and in much the same spirit, Calle Copernic ends in a staircase at the junction with Calle Galileo.

So, beware! You would be ill advised to drive down Calle Guido as it too ends in a staircase where it intersects with Calle Luis Agote.

NEARBY

MIGUEL ABUELO'S BENCH

La Isla has a flat area with a granite bench under a weeping willow. It is said to be the place where the famous Argentinian rock star Miguel Abuelo liked to sit for hours. Rumour has it that he recruited his musicians for Los Abuelos de la Nada here. It was in the days when hippy-like singers such as Abuelo and Tanguito could still sleep out in the open in the parks.

MUSEO DE CIENCIA Y TÉCNICA

Faculty of Engineering, Buenos Aires University
2214 Avenida Las Heras
• Metro: line D, Pueyrredon station
• Buses: 10, 37, 41, 60, 93, 102, 110
• Guided tours: 9am–7pm. Phone bookings only: + 54 11 4514-3003

A very confidential collection

Not many people are aware that the Faculty of Engineering of Buenos Aires University (UBA), or the "Gothic Cathedral" as it is also known, has a Museum of Science and Technology. Although it organises guided tours for secondary and high-school students and accepts phone bookings from the general public, the museum lacks staff and is therefore not keen to attract too many visitors.

There is a wide range of remarkable pieces on display, such as a clock by Foucault which is in working order, a lamp by Edison, a piece of Moon rock and a coil capable of producing a flash of light with a 0.5 million volt discharge.

On either side of the imposing staircase, visitors can admire a series of model boats, while a scaled-down steam locomotive, a display on the Pythagorean theorem and a replica of the Eiffel Tower are all part of the museum's permanent collection.

WHY IS THE "GOTHIC CATHEDRAL" UNFINISHED?

Visitors to the Museum of Science and Technology can tour the whole building with its imposing neo-Gothic interior, unique in Buenos Aires, even if it was never finished. In 1909 the architect Arturo Prins was chosen for the construction of the building: it was inaugurated in 1925, despite the fact that it was not yet finished. The building work then came to a halt and nothing more was done for ten years; the project was finally abandoned due to lack of funds in 1938. Prins died the following year and rumours began as to why the building work had been stopped: some said that it was due to an error in the calculations and that the fact of simply adding brick to the structure woul' have caused it to collapse. They said that the architect had committed suic' on realising what a foolish mistake he had made. The most plausible rea however, would seem to be that successive governments had quite s' shown no interest in the building.

MAUSOLEUM OF SEÑOR AND SEÑORA SALVADOR MARIA DEL CARRIL

(18)

Recoleta Cemetery
1760 Calle Junin
• Buses: 10, 37, 59, 92, 108, 124, 130

> *A couple who did not speak to each other for 21 years*

There is one particular mausoleum in Recoleta cemetery which will catch your eye. It belongs to Salvador Maria del Carril, who was vice-president under President General Justo José de Urquiza (1854–1860). The mausoleum is a real curiosity: Señora del Carril's bust turns its back on her husband's.

Salvador Maria del Carril, an unassuming and rather austere doctor, married Tiburcia Dominguez. Although they had seven children together and everything seemed in order, their marriage was not a happy one.

Del Carril's wife was a great spendthrift who frenetically bought dresses, perfume and jewellery regardless of their cost. She even went as far as changing all the furniture in the house on a whim. The doctor was so shocked by his wife's wasteful behaviour that he used his influence to get his domestic grievances published in the national press. He officially announced here that he would no longer bail her out or give her any further allowances. From one day to the next, Tiburcia was stripped of her status as a member of high society and was seen by all as an outright spendthrift.

Señora del Carril was so mortified by the way she had been treated, and so humiliated by the public scandal, that she decided never to talk to her husband again. They therefore did not speak to each other for twenty-one years until he died. Señora del Carril then took great pleasure in spending what remained of her late husband's fortune. What is more, unforgiving to the bitter end, she asked that the bust on her grave turn its back on her husband's. Even the sun only shines on one bust at a time while the other remains in the shadows, as if to remind us of the antagonism between the two estranged spouses.

DAVID ALLENO'S GRAVE

Recoleta cemetery
1760 Calle Junin
• Buses: 10, 37, 59, 60, 61, 92, 93, 102, 108

> *The man who committed suicide once his grave was ready*

David Alleno's grave is at the back of the Recoleta cemetery, in zone 20, near a wall running alongside Calle Azcuenaga. It has a tiny gravestone standing on the narrowest part of the plot, with a basic inscription ("David Alleno, cemetery warden from 1881 to 1910"), and is one of the cemetery's most intriguing graves.

The fascinating story behind it goes back to the end of the 19th century, when David, who was just 8 years old, started going to the cemetery with his older brothers who worked there as guards. He enjoyed wandering from grave to grave, among the vaults and the sculptures, memorising many of the inscriptions.

When David was old enough, he started work as a maintenance man. Later, in 1881, he became the cemetery warden. He never got married and chose to live in a room in a *conventillo* rather than having his own home. His only aim in life was to buy a plot in the cemetery where he could build his own grave.

Fortunately for him, one of his brothers won the lottery and decided to share his winnings with the rest of the family. With his share, David travelled to Italy to order a marble statue of himself and make his dream come true. The statue showed David in his work overalls and hat, with a watering can, a brush and a bunch of keys.

When he got back to Buenos Aires, he bought a plot measuring 2 x 1 metres and, as soon as the work was finished, he resigned from his job. He then went straight back to his room and shot himself in the head so that he could be laid to rest in the grave that he had made for himself.

The *conventillos* were cheap lodgings for the immigrants and impoverished families of Buenos Aires.

PIERRE BENOÎT'S TOMB

Recoleta cemetery
1760 Calle Junin
• Buses: 10, 17, 41, 37, 59, 60, 92, 102, 108, 110, 124, 130

> *Is the son of Marie Antoinette and Louis XVI buried in Recoleta cemetery?*

Pierre Benoît (1836–1897), the architect who drew up the plans for the city of La Plata, was buried in Recoleta cemetery next to his father, also called Pierre Benoît. Some say that the latter could well be the heir to the French throne …

To get to the bottom of this mystery, we must go back to 1792, when the Dauphin was locked away in the Temple prison in Paris: Louis-Charles of France, second son of Marie Antoinette and Louis XVI, was just 7 years old at the time. According to the history books, he died of tuberculosis in 1795. Another theory, however, argues that he took refuge in Buenos Aires, using personal references from Napoleon Bonaparte, and that he grew up there under the name of Pierre Benoît, having been adopted by a wealthy family.

The rest of the legend is surrounded in mystery and peppered with coincidences and omissions. People say that when Pierre Benoît got married and was asked to give his mother's name, he said that she was called Marie Antoinette and skilfully avoided giving his father's name. The great-granddaughter of Pierre Benoît, *fils* (the La Plata town planner), Elina Benoit Pieres, claimed: "The fact that my great-great-grandfather is Louis XVI has been passed down from generation to generation. He revealed his royal lineage to his daughter. He received letters in French but he refused to open them and allowed no one in the family to speak the language."

What we do know for sure is that when a body was exhumed from the Dauphin's grave in 1846 in the Sainte-Marguerite cemetery in Paris (see *Secret Paris* from the same publisher), it was not identified as being the remains of Louis-Charles: the body was that of a young man aged between 15 and 18, which did not correspond to the Dauphin's age in 1795.

The plot thickened yet again in 1996, when someone found the remains of Pierre Benoît, *père*, in a corner of the cemetery buried with those of eighteen other people. Scientific tests revealed that he had been poisoned with arsenic. Who on earth could have wanted to kill this unassuming engineer, who had been bedridden for years after having a stroke?

From that day onwards, the Benoît family has chosen not to comment.

MASONIC SYMBOLISM IN THE RECOLETA CEMETERY

1760 Calle Junin
- Open all year: 7am—5pm
- Metro: line D, Callao station
- Buses: 10, 37, 59, 108, 110, 124

> **Sarmiento, a well-known Argentinian Freemason, designed his very own tomb**

When visitors to the Recoleta Cemetery come in search of the more famous graves here, they often miss the Masonic symbols hidden among them.

In 1853 the famous necropolis was stripped of its Episcopal consecration when President Bartolomé Mitre ordered that the body of Dr Blas Aguerro, a well-known Freemason, be exhumed. The archbishop of Buenos Aires had refused to give him a Christian burial due to this allegiance.

The mausoleum of Domingo Faustino Sarmiento, who was one of Argentina's heroes and an important figure in the world of Freemasonry here, is worth a visit. He went as far as designing his very own tomb, scrupulously keeping track of the progress of the construction work even when on his travels. We know this from his letters to his sisters.

At the entrance of the cemetery, walk down to the end of the first alley on your left, where you will see a passageway just before you come to the wall. Here you will find a crypt covered in Masonic allegories. There is a remarkable pavement with black-and-white mosaics symbolising Darkness and Light, the Chain of Union and the Obelisk which represent the Stone of Perfection.

If you look carefully, you may spot a plaque from the Argentinian Lodge tucked away behind a pot – Sarmiento belonged to this lodge. The family mausoleum was completed in 1883, five years before he died. It was declared a listed national monument in 1946.

Another well-known pantheon is the "Obedience to the Law" Lodge, which is decorated with the Compass, the Set Square and the letter "G" – symbols which represent limits/borders, virtue and God, considered the Great Architect of the Universe. Perhaps the most famous of all these Masonic symbols, the Delta (representing the essence of divinity), proudly decorates the front of the mausoleum between the niches numbered 1–6 (section 11, zone 6) in the cemetery.

RUBBER TREE OF LA RECOLETA

Crossroads of Calles Roberto Ortiz and Quintana, Recoleta district
• Buses: 17, 60, 67, 110, 124

> **A tree
> of amazing
> proportions**

The city's oldest tree can be found on the Recoleta promenade in Plaza Juan XXIII. This imposing rubber tree, with its enormous branches and huge roots, stands next to a traditional sweet shop, La Biela.

The tree (botanical name: *Ficus elastica*) was brought back from India by Recollect monks in 1791 and planted by the agronomist Martin José de Altolaguirre on his farm, De La Recollera. It has certainly flourished since that time. Today the base of the trunk is 7 metres wide and it stretches up more than 20 metres into the sky. Some of its branches are over 25 metres long, giving it an overwhelming total span of 50 metres.

Healthy as it is, the tree's amazing proportions have needed props laid under its branches to avoid them cracking under the weight.

In 2014 a sculpture called *Atlas* by Joaquin Arbiza was erected under one of these heavy branches. The unfortunate titan is shown symbolically holding the history of the tree on his shoulders. The sculpture was made using scrap metal from old cars and is composed of 3,000 different pieces welded together. It stands 1.92 metres high and weighs 250 kg. Take a closer look and you will see some quirky details, such as the key of an old Argentinian Renault embedded in one of his arms.

Over the last 250 years, the rubber tree has witnessed the many social, cultural and urban changes that have gradually transformed Buenos Aires from its beginnings. Locals say that all the city's rubber trees come from cuttings of the original one.

ALTAR OF RELICS

Nuestra Señora del Pilar
1904 Calle Junín, Recoleta district
• Buses: 17, 61, 92, 110, 124
• Guided tours one Sunday every month
• For information, call + 54 11 4806 2209

> **The church
> holds the remains
> of St Peter
> and St Joseph**

The basilica of Nuestra Señora del Pilar (Our Lady of the Pillar) dates from the 18th century. It is the city's second oldest church (after St Ignatius, inaugurated in 1722) and the only colonial-style church that is still standing. Located in one of Buenos Aires' most popular tourist neighbourhoods, right next to the famous Recoleta cemetery, the church welcomes thousands of the faithful every year.

The cloisters, chapels, cistern patio and museum should not be missed. However, few people are aware that the "altar of relics" holds the remains of St Peter, St Joseph, St Anne, St Joachim, St Ignatius of Loyola and St John. Somewhat paradoxically, this remarkable secret, which is nevertheless on public view, is not signposted at all and often goes unnoticed.

The altar, which is situated on the right-hand side of the entrance, was specially constructed in 1779 to house the relics presented by King Charles III of Spain to Father Francisco de Altolaguirre, the first indigenous Recollect brother, who visited the Spanish king. Made of polychrome wood with tortoiseshell, bronze and pewter details, the reliquary contains an urn, liturgical objects and a large number of wax portraits.

On one side of the railings around the chapel, there are documents explaining the origins of the relics, including the dispatch notice that accompanied the shipment from Spain.

There is no mention, on the other hand, of the saints whose remains are said to lie under the arches of the church. According to the church authorities, this information comes from the Archivo General de Indias (General Archive of the Indies) in Seville. Created by the king in 1785, this institution holds all available information relating to the administration of the Spanish colonies, including a complete list of the martyrs whose remains were placed in the reliquary.

"TREE-DOOR" IN PLAZA SAN MARTIN DE TOURS

Avenidas Alvear and Adolfo Bioy Casares, Recoleta district
• Buses: 17, 67, 92, 93, 110, 124, 130

> *Breathing new life into dead trees*

In Plaza San Martin de Tours, in Recoleta district, there is a red door with a lock, carved into an old tree trunk.

The artist Diego Musadi and the muralist Alicia Quintana created this work of art. It was part of a joint project in 2001 to breathe new life into the dead trees on the square that were going to be chopped down.

The tree in question, which was "restored" and then painted, has become an intriguing sight for passers-by.

Another example of these two artists' work can be seen between the shops in Calle Juan B. Justo, at No. 6500: a door with a rather garish golden lock carved into a tree.

Musadi sees these works as a way of linking art with the environment and as an artistic means of recycling tree trunks that would otherwise be chopped up.

Most of the trees in Plaza San Martin de Tours were originally planted by Recollect monks in the 19th century. The most famous is the one standing on Avenida Alvear. It was donated by the then president, Nicolas Avellaneda, who was a keen amateur botanist. The tree is a giant *Ficus* dating back to the 19th century and has enormous maze-like roots.

OLD RECORDING STUDIO IN THE ATENEO GRAND SPLENDID

1860 Avenida Santa Fe, Barrio Norte district
- Metro: line D, Callao station
- Buses: 12, 39, 106, 111, 124, 150, 152

I n the famous Ateneo Grand Splendid bookshop, tucked away at the top of a small staircase, lies a somewhat oddly proportioned room (measuring 5 x 20 metres) that used to be a recording studio. It has a beautiful pinewood floor and is filled with light thanks to its large windows. How many

Where Gardel's voice became a legend in 1920

of the hundreds of visitors who browse through the bookshop's shelves know that the legendary tango singer, Carlos Gardel, recorded there for the Odeon record label, in spite of the often stifling heat?

Max Glücksman, Pathé's film distributor in Argentina, ordered the construction of the building. It stands in an area called Barrio Norte, previously known as the "Saint-Germain of Buenos Aires" in reference to the Bohemian atmosphere of the famous district in Paris. In 1919 Argentina's first cinema, the Cine Teatro Grand Splendid, built by the architects Pizoney and Falcope, opened here. The ornate fresco decorating the inside of the dome is the work of the Italian maestro Nazareno Orlandi.

The room where the old recording studio used to be is just behind this dome. There are many stories about what went on here: Glücksman is said to have been so passionate about tango that he went as far as advising Gardel on how to improve the quality of his voice during recording sessions. One of his techniques was to get the singer to lean on a chair to enlarge his thoracic cage.

Radio Splendid, one of Argentina's most popular radio stations, broadcast from here and it is also where Gardel started his career.

Unfortunately, this room is not open to the public today as it is used as a storeroom for the bookshop.

PATIO DEL LICEO

PACIO CREATIVO

SEJO GE
DIDADES
ONTRARA

PATIO DEL LICEO

2729 Avenida Santa Fe, Barrio Norte district
• Metro: line D, Agüero and Pueyrredon stations

> *A leafy
> green paradise
> where art, fashion
> and the avant-
> garde rule*

The Patio del Liceo is a strange place and the only one of its kind. It's a sort of green oasis which, like many other places in Buenos Aires, has a story all of its own. First it was a cemetery during the British invasions, then a high school for girls up to the 19th century. Finally, it was used as a shopping centre before being dismantled in 1995, due to in-house disputes.

At the beginning of 2006, a young lawyer, Herman Taraman, came across the place and bought up the shops little by little. In 2009 he undertook a renovation project with an architect, a project manager (Antonio Varela) and a couple of friends.

Today the walls of the Patio del Liceo are covered in graffiti and it has become a garden hidden away between Calles Anchorena and Laprida. Resident designers, up-and-coming artists and painters have opened up their workshops to the public in this leafy green paradise of fashion, art and the avant-garde.

The atmosphere is reminiscent of traditional Andalusian patios and among the galleries you will find Pasto y Fiebre (Studio 488), which showcases the work of young interior designers. There is also a bookshop, a rather original clothes shop and a designer jeweller, making the Patio one of the city's most creative underground spaces. And while you're there, why not linger a while longer, to try out Antonio Varela's delicious vegetarian cooking?

MAIN DOOR OF THE MUSEO CASA DE RICARDO ROJAS

2837 Calle Charcas
• Metro: line D, Agüero station

The home of Ricardo Rojas has been converted into the Museum House of Ricardo Rojas and research institute. This essay-writer and educator (1882–1957) came from Tucumán Province. This would explain the façade's exact resemblance to that of the historic Casa de Tucumán, where Argentina's independence from Spain was declared on 9 July 1816.

An identical façade to that of the Casa de Tucumán

Rojas, who also wrote a biography of José San Martin (1778–1850), the Argentinian general and hero of independence, grew up near the House of Miguel of Tucumán. When planning the construction of his home many years later in Buenos Aires, he therefore naturally wanted it to be built in the same neocolonial style, with rooms running off a large, central patio. He lived here from 1929 until his death in 1957. A year later, his widow, Maria Julieta Quinteros de Rojas, donated the house to the State, along with the furniture, works of art and huge bookcases. In 1958 the house was officially added to the List of National Museums.

Thanks to the detailed restoration work carried out on the building in 2013, the original main door has been preserved. Its Inca-style decorations and distinctly Peruvian-inspired style form a stark contrast with today's resolutely modern urban landscape.

SOUTH

MANOBLANCA MUSEUM

❶

Tabaré 1371, Pompeya
• Mon-Fri 8.30-11am and 2-4pm • Free entry
• Guided tours: reservations tel. +54 11 4918 9448

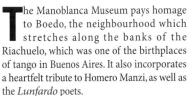

*Buenos
Aires' temple
of fileteado*

The Manoblanca Museum pays homage to Boedo, the neighbourhood which stretches along the banks of the Riachuelo, which was one of the birthplaces of tango in Buenos Aires. It also incorporates a heartfelt tribute to Homero Manzi, as well as the *Lunfardo* poets.

Born thirty years ago out of the determination of the collector don Gregorio Plotnicki, the museum contains a variety of exhibits: paintings, photographs, busts, portraits of the most familiar images associated with tango, etc. Visitors will also see coins, stamps, archives from the area, antiques, miniatures and other trinkets, all of which evoke memories of a bygone era.

The section dedicated to *fileteado* (a style of decorative painting and drawing typical of Buenos Aires) is worth a visit in its own right. *Fileteado* developed in the 19th-century as a form of decoration for animal-drawn carriages used to transport foodstuffs and was later expanded to include Mercedes-Benz *colectivos* (buses).

The Manoblanca Museum possesses a very large collection of *fileteados*, many of which were decorated by the most famous artists, such as León Untroib, Martiniano Arce and Luis Sorz. It is thus known today as the *fileteado* museum, as it is the only one in the city. In fact, this original art form was not recognised as being part of Buenos Aires' cultural heritage until the 1970s.

The museum is open to visitors from Monday to Friday, during the early part of the morning and in the afternoon. The tour commentary is provided by the museum host, who is also responsible for maintenance and looking after each room. The museum closes at week-ends so that don Gregorio can take a well-earned break.

FRAGMENTS OF THE BERLIN WALL

Building of the Perfil publishing house
2715 Calle California, Retiro district
• Roca train line, Hipolito Yrigoyen station
• Buses: 10, 12, 17, 20, 22, 24, 45, 74, 93, 129, 134
Palacio San Martín, 761 Calle Arenales, Montserrat district
• Metro: line C, San Martín station
• Buses: 45, 106, 108, 150, 152

> *One of the largest fragments to have left Germany*

The city of Buenos Aires has in its possession two pieces of universal modern-day history: two fragments of the Berlin Wall that are on display in the Retiro and Montserrat neighbourhoods.

This iconic symbol of a divided world during the Cold War came tumbling down in the afternoon of 9 November 1989, after having stood for twenty-eight years. Fragments of the wall were then handed out to over forty countries, including Argentina.

At the Chacabuco and Diagonal intersection, you can't miss the huge concrete wall covered in graffiti, looming up on the side of the entrance hall of the Perfil building. It is one of the largest fragments of the wall on display outside Germany today and was made with a row of seven blocks, which can be seen from the pavement outside.

José Fontevecchia, Perfil's director, said they had thought about acquiring a fragment of the wall on the day it fell: "We were about to launch a new magazine called *Noticias* and we thought it would be a great symbol for freedom of speech." The journalist contacted the German embassy to see if it would be possible to acquire a piece of the wall: a week later he was told that it would … if they agreed to fund the construction of a school in Germany. The cost of building the school ($10,000 at the time) was nothing compared with that of bringing the blocks from Germany to Argentina in 1992. *Noticias* was then able to stick tiny fragments of the wall into their magazines to give their readers a small piece of modern history.

The San Martín Palace, seat of the Argentinian Chancellery, also has a piece of the Berlin Wall inserted into its own garden wall. This piece was given by the German government to commemorate the tenth anniversary of the fall of the wall. Although this concrete block is much smaller (measuring only 3 metres high and 1.20 metres long) than the piece in Calle Chacabuco, its presence here is highly symbolic. It is an emblem of liberty and of the unity of nations. The San Martín Palace conducts regular free tours of the gardens.

EL COLOSO DE AVELLANEDA SCULPTURE

Camino de la Ribera, intersection of Calles Pellegrini and Laval,
Avellaneda district
• Buses: 10, 17, 22, 33, 74, 95, 98, 100, 134

> **Monument to the "shirtless"**

On the outskirts of the city, an oxidised metal statue, in honour of workers, rises 15 metres high over the factories in the industrial zone situated on the banks of the Riachuelo. It commemorates 17 October 1945, when workers marched on the capital in support of Juan Domingo Perón (1895–1974), who had been imprisoned by the dictatorship. This is the most significant workers' uprising in Argentina's history to date.

The sculpture is by Alejandro Marmo (famous for his work using industrial waste in public places) and Daniel Santoro, a painter who was inspired by Peronist iconography. Entitled "*The Colossus of Avellaneda*", it was erected discreetly in May 2013.

The same artists made two other metal sculptures representing Evita which are on the Public Works building on Avenida 9 de Julio (see p. 75).

Marmo describes his "shirtless" figure as "retro-futurist": "The scrap metal from factories is a perfect metaphor for several images at once: the uprooted immigrant and his gloomy thoughts, the chimney smoke and the typical sight of workers sitting on the pavement eating their lunch …". The impressive figure seems to be wading out of the troubled waters of the Riachuelo.

The monument is in a very quiet place, on the riverbank. To get a better look, you will need to cross over the bridge and admire it from Avenida Don Pedro de Mendoza. The statue faces the town and holds Evita's head in its hands. The inscriptions on one of its legs appear to be random dates, but in fact represent key periods in Argentina's history: the popular uprising in Cordoba in 1969; the workers' strikes in 1982; 19 and 20 December 2001, when two successive governments were overthrown; and, last but not least, 17 October 1945.

THE COLOURFUL FACADES OF CALLE LANIN ❹

33 Calle Lanin, Barracas district
• Buses: 25, 45, 95, 100, 134

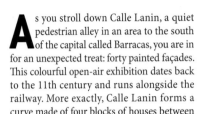

The road where psychedelia rules

As you stroll down Calle Lanin, a quiet pedestrian alley in an area to the south of the capital called Barracas, you are in for an unexpected treat: forty painted façades. This colourful open-air exhibition dates back to the 11th century and runs alongside the railway. More exactly, Calle Lanin forms a curve made of four blocks of houses between Calle Suarez and Calle Bransen.

The project began in 2001, when residents and artists began painting the façades at a local street party. Four years later, they were joined by a local mosaic artist. Marino Santa Maria, a visual artist, designed the decorations on all of the façades. He was born and raised in the district and wanted to transform the grey industrial zone into a public arts space, thus improving its previously poor image.

In 1998 Santa Maria began by painting the front of his house. Then primary colours were used to decorate the others in his street, every design being adapted to the architectural style of each individual house. Local residents played an essential role in the development of the project, some of them even painting their own façades.

For Santa Maria, the aim of this project is neither to transform the street into an open-air museum nor to create a new Caminito. What he really hopes is that this road manages to keep its vibrant spirit so that art and the bustle of everyday life may live alongside each other: "Public art is not supposed to have a function; it is just there to give people who cannot go to museums a chance to experience culture."

FENCE OF SANTA FELICITAS CHURCH

520 Calle Isabel la Católica, Barracas district
• Buses: 12, 17, 24, 39, 45, 60, 93, 129
• Annual ceremony on 30 January

Every year on 30 January, the fence surrounding Santa Felicitas Church in the Barracas area is covered in ribbons and white or red handkerchiefs: the legend goes that anyone who takes hold of the gate will meet the love of their life, or if they have already done so, they will stay together for ever.

Those who leave a handkerchief will meet the love of their life

The story behind the legend, however, would seem to be more about thwarted than eternal love.

Despite being beautiful and rich, Felicitas Guerrero was unhappy. When she was 15 her father married her off to Martin de Alzaga, who was three times her age. She bore him two children: one died of yellow fever at the age of 6 and the other died a short time after he was born. When her husband died a few years later, Felicitas found herself besieged by admirers, all wanting to get their hands on her and her fortune. One of them, Enrique Ocampo, an aristocrat, was so obsessed with Felicitas that he stalked her day and night. He vowed that if he could not have her love, then he would show her his darker side. Realising that she would never love him, this is exactly what he did: he shot her in the back and killed her on 30 January 1872.

The Guerrero family had a church built in memory of the young woman on the very spot where the fateful event took place and this is how the legend began: because of her murderer's curse, Felicitas could not rest in peace and it is said that her ghost can sometimes be seen roaming around the church.

Local churchgoers, however, see her as a soul in search of redemption. This is why, on the anniversary of her death, the gate is covered in ribbons and handkerchiefs left behind by the unfortunate. Some people even go as far as hanging on to the gate in the hope that it will help them to meet the love of their life.

Santa Felicitas is the last German neo-romantic church still standing today. It is also the only church in Buenos Aires to have statues representing terrestrial figures. This imposing and decidedly eclectic building was designed by the architect Ernesto Bunge and also has some Gothic influences. Two large marble statues greet visitors as they enter: on the right, a standing figure of Martin de Alzaga; and on the left, Felicitas with one of her children. The busts of the young woman's parents are in the sacristy.

A MONUMENT TO LIONS

6

100 Calle Montes de Oca, Barracas district
- Buses: 4, 12, 29, 53, 60, 134, 154, 168
- Metro: line C, Constitucion station
- Train: Roca line, Constitucion station

> *The bizarre story of four pet lions*

There is an intriguing statue adorning the house at No. 100 in Calle Montes de Oca. It shows a lion devouring a man. The story behind this statue is so bizarre that it has become something of a legend. It is said that a capricious millionaire adopted four lions and kept them as pets.

The manor house, which stands in the southern area of the city, is built to look like a haunted house, a style made popular by the French in the 19th century. It belonged to Eustaquio Diaz Vélez, a member of the local bourgeoisie who had more than enough money to satisfy his eccentric whims. His father had fought in the army, defending Argentina against the British, but Eustaquio, who often dreamed of the African savannah, was interested in nothing but big cats.

Foolishly, he acquired four African lions and locked them in cages placed in his garden. As you may imagine, they gave his guests a real fright. Little did he know that their presence was to have serious consequences for his very own family. One evening, he invited over 100 guests to the engagement party of one of his daughters. A lion managed to escape from a cage that had not been securely fastened. The story goes that the lion jumped out of the bushes onto the husband-to-be while the rings were being exchanged. The lion's owner rushed to get his gun and shot the animal, but it was too late. The young man died and his daughter was so distraught that she committed suicide a month later.

Don Eustaquio had the other three lions put down but he was so passionate about big cats that he couldn't resist having a sculpture made, representing the tragic scene.

Ironically, the house is now the head office of an association that looks after and provides work for people with physical disabilities.

SAN JOSÉ OBSERVATORY

④

2455 Bartolome Mitre, Once district
- Guided tours: Fri 8pm–10pm
- Bookings: +54 949510264/4303
- Astronomy lessons for all ages over 12

> *A strategic military observation post during the 1880 and 1890 Revolutions*

In the Once neighbourhood there is a domed tower, symbolising the metamorphosis undergone by Buenos Aires in the last century. It was erected in 1870 among a group of buildings including San José College and Notre-Dame of Balvenera Church.

At that time, all the important monuments were built to include some kind of watchtower. The one in San José College is undoubtedly one of the most impressive. Its base measures 6 x 5 metres and it was exceptionally high for its time (about 25 metres), with five floors. A crenellated border around the top makes it look like a medieval guard tower.

The tower's high vantage point meant that it became a strategic observation post during the 1880 and 1890 Revolutions. It was also the city's first astronomic observatory and remained in use up to the 1970s. It was then closed and abandoned until 1981, when a group of teachers and pupils from San José College decided to climb up to its attic. Much to their surprise, they came across an antique bronze astronomic telescope made by the French manufacturer Mailhat.

The telescope was completely renovated (the original mechanism was replaced by a synchronous electric motor) and, a year later, it was back in use. The tower is now open to the public as an amateur observatory and the telescope will soon celebrate its centenary.

On your way up the tower, you will walk along corridors that are more than 150 years old. Once at the very centre of the building, get ready for a long climb. A narrow stairway (about ten floors high) leads to the top of the tower. A word of advice if you want to make it to the top: take a little time to catch your breath and admire the portraits of the more illustrious names in the history of astronomy – Ptolemy, Copernicus and Kepler – hanging on the walls on the way up.

WEATHERVANE OF CABALLITO

Plaza Caballito
130 Calle Rojas
• Metro: line A, Primera Junta station
• Train: Sarmiento line, Caballito station

Many people would be surprised to know that it is the small metal figure standing in the middle of Plaza Caballito that gave its name to the district.

The symbol that gave its name to the district

In 1821 an immigrant from Genoa, Nicola Vila, bought the block of houses formed by Calles Juan Bautista Alberdi, Rivadavia, Emilio Mitre and Victor Martinez.

He then built a four-roomed house there and set up a bar in one of the rooms.

Just opposite this bar, which was called Don Nicola, he erected a ship's mast topped with the silhouette of a horse.

The front of the bar looked out onto Camino Real, today known as Avenida Rivadavia. Its ideal location meant that it soon became a popular bar for locals, who called it the "bar of the little horse".

In 1858 the train station was named Caballito (Little Horse), a name that has survived to the present day.

After Don Nicola was killed in a burglary, his son took over the business until the building was eventually split up. As for the horse, a replica was made and it was erected in Plaza Primera Junta.

Since 2009, however, another copy of the little symbol has been standing in Plaza Caballito on a well-kept lawn near the railway tracks.

The original weathervane is on display in the Museo Histórico y Colonial in Lujan.

STATUES WALK

⑪

Avenidas San Juan and Boedo
• Metro: line E, Boedo station

*An
open-air
art exhibition*

In 2004 the Local History Society launched a project to erect ten statues along Avenida Boedo (from Calle Independencia to Avenida San Juan). These statues can now be seen standing on the pavements between the shops.

At No. 853, for example, there is a statue called *La Cholita*. It represents a typical village woman from the north of Argentina, sculpted in a granite-like material. It was donated by Francisco Reyes, an adopted *Porteño* (the term used for an inhabitant of Buenos Aires) of Spanish origin. He had arrived in Argentina at the age of 12 and later became an active member of a cultural movement in the suburbs.

The area around Avenidas San Juan and Boedo is named after the famous composer Homero Manzi, as it is one of the areas where the tango became popular. The row of statues, more or less hidden in between the shops, may be less noticeable than certain features of the more standard *tanguero* tours. Contemporary art has, however, played an important role in the area for some time. In the 1930s it was home to many sculptors – their works are included in the guided art tours on offer today and form an interesting contrast with the many electrical-appliance shops that have since set up business.

Walk further along to No. 943 and you will come to a statue called *Reposo,* the work of a Russian artist named Estephan Erzia. He came to Buenos Aires in 1927 to set up an exhibition and ended up staying in Argentina for twenty years.

Just opposite, there is a statue called *Testimonio,* created by the sculptor Alberto Balleti in homage to those who fell in the Falklands/Malvinas War.

A little further down the road stands *Tango íntimo* by Leo Vinci, representing two sensually entwined dancers: a decidedly emblematic statue for an area with such a tango-orientated background.

Of all the works, the most remarkable is undoubtedly *Interiores.* Look through the slot in the middle of the statue and you'll see Boedo in a whole new light.

EVANGELICAL CHRISTIAN CHURCH

5850 Calle Tinogasta, Villa Real district
• Buses: 21, 28, 47, 53, 80, 85, 108, 109, 117

A transparent and colourful place of worship

The "transparent church", as its congregation calls it, is an Evangelical church designed to depict two hands coming together in prayer. What is taking place inside can be seen from without, through the stained-glass structure. The official name is the Evangelical Christian Church. It was designed by the architect Murillo Luque, who used concrete and glass to allow a maximum amount of light into the building.

It was the members of the congregation who joined forces to help build their church. Some actually became involved in the building work while others organised fund-raising events, selling clothes and food to buy materials for the construction project. It took them a year to build the church (1969–1970).

Evangelists were present in the working-class Villa Real district as far back as 1931, when José Bongorra moved there with his fellow brothers to set up a small community with the help of the Villa Huro parish. Eight years later, the community – which only had 40 members – declared itself an independent church.

Bongorra helped Villa Real to take part in the first Evangelical Congress. The number of worshippers swelled to such an extent that, shortly afterwards, the church had to move to No. 5400 Calle Simbron. At that time, the worshippers only congregated on Saturdays, but in 1943 they moved on again to Calle Tinogasta, where the church (which now has a capacity of 2,000 seats) is located today.

NO. 1232 IN CALLE ECHENAGUCIA **⑪**

1232 Calle Echenagucia, Versailles district
• Buses: 47, 106, 108, 109

> *The house*
> *where* **Waiting for**
> **the Hearse**
> *was filmed*

The cult Argentinian film *Esperando la carroza* (Waiting for the Hearse) was shot in a typically Buenos Aires-style "*chorizo* house" (see box), at No. 1232 Calle Echenagucia. The actors Antonio Gasalla, China Zorrilla, Juan Manuel Tenuta and Luis Brandoni starred in this film alongside the owners of the house, who put in an appearance as extras.

The house was built in 1929 by a Spanish immigrant as a family home and remained untouched after the film was shot in March 1985 by Alejandro Doria. In 2011 some of neighbours got together to set up a support committee to prevent the place from being pulled down and to start renovating it. A local lawyer was quoted as saying: "Everyone, from the neighbours to the local shopkeepers, the ironmongers and the local tip, lent a hand in the restoration work."

Today, classic lines from the film can be heard echoing in the courtyard of the brightly coloured house and it now has a commemorative plaque. Just ring the bell if you'd like to know more about the shooting of the film or to take a photo of the place that journalists have called "a symbol of national identity". Recently the house was officially declared part of the Cultural Heritage of the City of Buenos Aires.

The film *Esperando la carroza* was adapted from the play of the same name, written in 1974 by the Uruguayan playwright Jacobo Langsner.

PLAZOLETA DE LOS CAMPEONES

9000 Calle Juan B. Justo
• Buses: 8, 16, 34, 47, 53, 99, 108

A little square (with a million-year-old stone) that is always closed

Visitors to the José Amalfitani stadium, home of Velez Sarsfield Football Club, will see what is possibly the city's smallest garden. The name given to this tiny square, however, is not what you would expect: Plazoleta de los Campeones (Champions Square). You may well wonder why this round, symbolically ball-shaped area remains mysteriously under lock and key.

Take a closer look from the outside and you may see a rock weighing 2,400 kg which was brought here from San Juan Province to the Liniers area and is said to be around a million years old.

The directors of the club (presided over for many years by José Amalfitani) were looking for a way to celebrate its centenary – they decided that the million-year-old rock was just what was needed. The square and the rock were therefore duly inaugurated in 2010 for this occasion.

This piece of the club's history celebrates its founders and fans with the inscription: "To its founders, its directors and its men and women".

Oddly enough, the only people who have since been allowed access to this tiny, locked-up square are the club's football stars.

CALESITA OF DON LUIS

5990 Avenida Ramón L. Falcón

> *Don Luis,*
> *the man*
> *who devoted*
> *his life to children*

It is impossible to miss the carousel of Don Luis: rising above a wall of painted bricks, it still stands on the site where it was erected, at the corner of Avenida Falcón and Calle Miralla. The national "Mr Carousel" day is celebrated every year on 4 November (his birthday), in honour of this man who devoted his life to children. He is so famous that a Facebook page* has been set up for him, full of anecdotes and moving messages. Indeed, everyone in the neighbourhood has a story to tell about this local character whose famous carousel has delighted four generations of children.

Initially, the carousel operated at the corner of Avenida Juan B. Justo and Fragueiro, and then in other streets in the Villa Luro and Liniers neighbourhoods, until Luis decided to set up permanently on the patio of his own house, where it still operates today, even though he died in 2013.

Luis Rodriguez entered this trade when his father, Juan, bought a second-hand carousel in March 1920, with money that had been lent to him. Juan was a former ticket inspector on the trams, but he wanted to work for himself in order to support his family. His horse, Rubio, which acted as the merry-go-round's engine, made it turn in time to the music from a barrel organ. At the age of 9, young Luis abandoned his studies to go into business with his father.

Juan died in 1944 and Luis continued to travel around with his carousel, like a circus ringmaster. Rubio had been replaced several years previously by a petrol-driven engine, followed by an electric motor. However, the structure itself and the original wooden horses remained the same, as did the cars, camels and planes that Don Luis built with his own hands. This corner on Avenida Falcón and Calle Miralla is now part of the city's historical heritage.

* https://www.facebook.com/calesitadonluis/

SCULPTURE OF *"EL GAUCHO RESERO"*

2300 Avenida Lisandro de la Torre, Mataderos district
• Buses: 55, 63, 92, 126, 180

> **How does a gaucho's horse walk?**

On Paseo Liborio Pupillo, Avenida Lisandro de la Torre (just opposite the Liniers Market), stands a sculpture that is the pride of the Mataderos neighbourhood: the *"Gaucho Resero"*. It was sculpted in bronze by Emilio Sarniguet and represents a horseman herding cattle and riding at a slow walk, the reins loose.

Surprisingly, despite the fact that this sculpture adorned the 10-peso coins of the national currency from 1963 to 1968, it stirred up a heated controversy.

Some said that the animal had a strange way of walking: the horse's legs move together symmetrically (the right front and hind legs go forwards together and the left front and hind legs go backwards together), whereas the front and hind pairs of a walking horse's legs would naturally move together diagonally (i.e. the right front leg with the hind left, and the left front leg with the hind right).

In spite of the criticisms, specialists all praise the realism of the statue. (When Sarniguet was commissioned to do the sculpture, he went to an *estancia* [ranch] in Ayacucho, in the Province of Buenos Aires, so that he could observe his models up-close.)

So why does the horse walk like this? Here's the secret: *gaucho reseros* traditionally ride horses that are trained to walk at a special gait called "ambling" (*pasuco* in Spanish). This is a symmetrical walk because the horse walks using its lateral pairs of legs, which is considered incorrect in the traditional equestrian world. The gauchos, however, train their horses specially to do this as it makes for a more comfortable ride, especially over long distances.

ALPHABETICAL INDEX

ALPHABETICAL INDEX